IBERIAN CLAIM

IBERIAN CLAIM

BY VINCENT CASCIANI

NEW DEGREE PRESS

IBERIAN CLAIM

ISBN

978-1-63730-460-0   *Paperback*
978-1-63730-577-5   *Kindle Ebook*
978-1-63730-578-2   *Ebook*

For Brian Sarmiento, Marcella Rust, and Anita Parker,

Thank you for inspiring me to write

Table of Contents

Author's Note

When I was in the sixth grade, I was assigned a project on an early American explorer. I picked Álvar Núñez Cabeza de Vaca because his name made me laugh. A month after my project was due, however, his story would not leave me alone; my twelve year-old humor had given way to a genuine interest in the man and his life. That summer, after I finished a hundred pages of a novelized version of his life, I suddenly realized that I would need to do actual research. I learned the hard way how to write a novel. I spent the next five months researching online and reading Núñez's firsthand account, knowing I would refer back to these sources endlessly. I erased those first hundred pages and began again.

Seven years later, this book has come together.

The following is the true story of one of American history's greatest culture clashes. After seeing success elsewhere in the Americas, the overconfident Spaniards underestimated both the people and terrain they planned to subjugate: the results were disastrous. This is a rare account of colonizers being humbled by their would-be colony. May it stand alongside the many stories of overpowering thieves claiming what is not theirs. The Spaniards that survived this endeavor, Álvar Núñez included, were completely transformed by their failures.

I have adhered mostly to what I know to be history; the added flourishes are dialogue, character depth, a tightened plot, and some additional interactions. Many of the events you will read are remarkable. These remarkable parts, the things you might have a hard time believing, are all taken from Álvar Núñez's personal account. His part in the course of history, which I have tried to keep intact, was to demonstrate the damage caused by selfish ambitions.

Layer by layer, I have grown closer to understanding why this story is so important. A parable has emerged for the way power works when power structures are ill-defined.

There are other directions I could have taken, but I was not the best suited to take those directions. I am not a professor, or a historian, or a member of an indigenous community. I wrote what I was knowledgeable and passionate about, and I believe that this book has a value separate from the voice of its writer. My hope is that these pages will provide you with entertainment and a new perspective.

Best,

Vincent Casciani

February 13th, 2021

PART ONE

IBÉRICO

CHAPTER 1

The Motive

ALVAR NÚÑEZ

A Spanish Prison, 1545

Ambition is not what led me to this cell.

Ambition is instead the mark of my ancestors, the trait which passed through my family's generations. Ambition granted me my life's earliest successes, but it did not drive me into prison. No, that was something else. Men who act from ambition live freely. They either own the world or plan to own it. I know that well, and for most of my years that knowledge fueled me. These false charges, though, are not the product of such a motive. Compassion, rather, brought me here. Sympathies wore into me so thoroughly that I allowed my knees to buckle.

The pen is my last attempt at restoration. I wish to leave a testament of my true character. I will write clearly, carefully, and with the pointed honesty of a man who knows his defense will never work.

I certainly have much to defend against. *Treason*, the colonists had said, *corruption. A man who gives colonial funding to those dogs is not fit to serve. He grants the indígenas claims on churches and farming acres faster than our own landowners. Who knows how long it will be before they usurp us? And when they come, with their spears and axes, will he defend us? Of course not! He's a coward, a native-lover, a man who lets them work for their living and still feels sorry. Unnatural, disgraceful to let them walk around with so few boundaries. We'd be better for a man like Núñez to rot.*

He's guilty. Send him back across the ocean and let the Spanish courts handle him.

"It's rationing," I argued. "Not corruption. They get no pay for their work; the land we cut out for them can't even be farmed. They have no doctors; when they get sick, they drop like flies, when all that's needed is medicine."

I reasoned, I pined, I appealed to them. But it was fruitless.

"Is it treason to let them live?" My last appeal.

"Treason is to hurt the interest of the Spanish throne." Their firm response.

Here, sitting on this cell's bench, my bare feet on crude cobblestones, I stare at the pen, ink, and paper provided by the guard. I must regain my honor. But I have already lost; the world is convinced, and I am already serving my time.

I cannot save my honor, but I can still mark my legacy. My story deserves to be told. The mission which earned me my name posed a challenge to ambition far greater than any years in prison. I will write for as long as I am in chains. My story will clear my name in the only way that counts.

I was young when I decided to be a soldier. I was not especially interested in the military. But as the youngest of four brothers—all of whom had served before me in the wake of my grandfather's insatiable, gallivanting memory—I knew little else. The eldest of my brothers had died already, the youngest was discharged for irreparable injury, and the middle brother still held his place in the infantry of an Italian war. I joined the army at fifteen and earned my first honors at twenty-two. I served a loosely-bound nation, held together only by a politically-motivated marriage, whose strength and longevity no sane man could trust. Nevertheless, my own Castilian Queen offered her men to the Aragónese King as ammunition. The Pope approved the arrangement and thus this union became the Mediterranean military engine, devouring territory for the new Spanish throne and the tastes of the Vatican. And the military engine worked.

It was within this engine that my mind was reformed, given a twisted slant.

When the territory ran out and the Castilian Queen died, the battles ended, and I, a twenty-five year-old, was left with nothing ahead of me but the life of a retired soldier. This brought me no peace. Like all others at the time, I feared for Spanish stability. Would the union hold without its matriarch? Would the King grow into a tyrant and replace the Queen's Castilla with the culture and language of his Aragón? Alas, not much changed. The disjointed unity persisted. I and the Castilians were quite relieved, while the Aragónese didn't much care one way or the other.

But whatever we were, beyond our political concerns, we had been marked indelibly by the battlefield. The battlefield had been the only object for our youthful drive. It had turned our youth into force, our ignorance into bravery. Yet the battles were over, at least in the common man's narrow scope; without an outlet, our ambitions festered until they became bitter vices, focused inward to our homesteads and communities. My particular childhood home was a town in the southernmost point of Iberia. However, I married and moved north to work as a civil officer in Sevilla, where the street squabbles needed minding and the popular order needed to be spoken for. What an insular life it was. Every social function and meal in the kindly-rummed Duke's home was a blow to my manhood. I possessed, as of then, insignificant land, no title, no noble name, and I would never climb the ranks of their rusting ladder. But to abandon the ladder was to vine my outer walls, and I surely could not let myself starve. Public life, my life, was a farce I faced with self-sustaining denial.

"You know what, Nuñez," a local merchant said. "Why not ship out to the Indies? It would probably wipe that frown off your face and give you something to do."

"No, thanks," I said. "I have a wife and home to tend to."

"Are you sure?" The Sevillan merchant smiled coyly. "I can see it in your eyes, the urge to leave."

I handed him his money. "I'm very sure of myself. And I'm sure your business would do better if you weren't so distracted with mine." The merchant nodded without responding.

My wife, however, gave me nothing in the way of assurance.

"Tell me," she would say, "about what you did today." I would tell her about the menial this and the ever-so-cumbersome that, and her slender face would scrunch together in repugnance. Then she'd smile, trying to temper her annoyance, and say "how wonderful" and quickly turn away to attend to her own mundane tasks (though she regularly boasted of their relative importance). I'd find her in such high spirits throughout the day, though when she'd notice me enter the door, her shoulders would drop and her airs would sink to guarded discomfort. Of course this left me weaker, with only the memory of when I had won her love. She had married a warrior, a man strong enough to satisfy her notions of what a woman deserved. But in our settled life my edge had dulled, and what I set my eyes toward was often clouded and unworthy of her praise. Her ideal of me as a husband was shattered by years of inescapable monotony. Granted, it was a monotony which served the same civil goals that the infantryman fought for, but without the glory. This seeming lack left a stifling hunger for all fickle, easily romanticized deviants. Of which María was one.

"Alvar," she said to me one spring morning, "why don't you bring flowers like Juan Velázquez? He always brings flowers to the rancher's daughter" (The rancher being our rich neighbor whose land was not far). "And he always smiles at me and says hello when I visit Yadira on the days he is courting her." She took a purposeful pause. "You know, if I was the rancher's daughter, I'm sure he would bring me flowers. He might as well be telling me as much." She smiled keenly at her wrist, then quickly gave me a sour look. "He gives a good appreciation of my presence, you know. And as a still-pretty woman, it's only right I get that. Just so you're aware."

María breathed, triumphant, and yet the casual observer would be wrong to believe she had finished. I interrupted before her discourse could go on unnipped.

"But, María, I did get you flowers. I bought them and brought them here and gave them to you with a smile; but you said 'No, Alvar, these are outrageously expensive,' and you refused to take care of the home until I convinced the seller to take them back. You said 'I won't provide my role if you're straying this far in providing your own. You're a man, you should think.' That is what you said."

At this María certainly lost her words, stumped, and it took a few moments for her to find the footing of another point against me. But I responded again before she could speak. "And so the next time, I learned from my mistake, and I picked you a handful of flowers myself from the field. And I brought them to you and told you they had been picked, but again you said 'No, Alvar, what were you thinking? You picked the Spanish sweet peas, and people would much rather see those in the ground.'" I looked at María with a probing righteousness and she huffed. But I finished regardless. "So you can't say I haven't brought you flowers like that young horseman. I have."

At last she said, "Yes, you may have; but never with gusto."

A week later the atmosphere in our house had become so uninhabitable that I determined to end her dissatisfaction. So I did not buy, or pick, but acquired flowers from a civil serviceman of the town who had owed me a favor. They were wild lilies. I hid them from María that night until the right moment, and then revealed them and their origins to her in full detail. She was elated, truly, and we made love in a better way than for a long while. In the morning, I expected much of that elation to carry over; yet instead, she returned with the same bitterness and with new reason. She said I hadn't once spoken her name in our passions and that she was sure a more loving man would say his woman's name in passion at least once. I had profaned her.

So it was then that I stopped endeavoring to end her dissatisfaction. María was lost in the remembrance of the younger me, a man who had passions. Could I ever live up to my own ghost? My wife had become a stain, a challenge to my very worth. If I ever was to restore a sense of purpose, I would have to prove her wrong. I needed to rediscover my passions and direction in life.

In the days that followed, I often came home to find María crying or sitting silently. She left her duties unattended. It was her only form of protest. Perhaps she wanted me to leave.

While at work, I heard louder rumblings of a place where a man could expend his energy, far outside the suppressive reach of civil order.

"Oh, don't pay that any mind, Núñez," the Duke said. "It's nothing but a savage land; only the classless types would waste their time." Europe was to him the only place that deserved a working hand.

"Not so," the Sevillan merchant later told me. "The West has gold and good soil, all of it ripe for the taking. Only a fool would leave that ripened fruit hanging from the tree."

The sailors and soldiers similarly spoke of the Americas with wide eyes, and it sparked in me a renewed fire of determination. I saw them leave, month by month before each winter, taking with them little but the same fire that begged me to abandon my current yoke and follow. First it had been Cristóbal Colón, devouring the Indies at the time of my birth; then it had been the early conquistadores, claiming other regions with the sharp tools best designed for claiming a home. Most recently it had been Cortés, so swift and adept that he conquered the greatest native army with nothing more than a ship's cavalry and a few convincing words. Now he was so powerful that not even the Throne could challenge his dominion without losing their men and honor. If Cortés could conquer a land and rule it unbothered, then any man with the strength to take over, as well as the ambition to keep his claim, could travel the waters and eat the fruit waiting to be picked. That was a power unmatched by most kings. The West was a call too prime not to answer, and so I joined a fleet and answered it.

CHAPTER 2

Wilderness

——

ALONSO DEL CASTILLO

La Florida Territory, 1528

It was spring, it was humid, and the crew hadn't been on the Peninsula for more than a week. Núñez hacked away at the branches in our path; down they came, his well-worn knife our guide to the camps ahead. Smoke rising above the trees was the only signal to follow, and there was nobody more than the two of us. We had no map. We had no horses. And as for me, I had no boots. The more we moved, the more my socks absorbed stale water; each time I peered above, the smoke had thinned even more. A burdening wetness bogged my feet by the time it fully dissipated.

"The smoke's gone," I said.

Núñez lowered his knife and turned around. He was partially kempt, with eyes that seemed never to blink. His were red where they should have shone white.

"We don't need the smoke."

He coughed and went back to hacking the branches.

Núñez, the squat bear of a man, had left Spain a Lieutenant; but being from a small number in the crew with credible military acclaim—and with some brains to complement it, I had heard—he soon saw a promotion. Captain Núñez. A tight group of such captains operated directly beneath the Governor, and whenever he had duties elsewhere, each controlled their smaller section in the expedition. It was a pseudo-military devised to maintain some order. But the Governor rarely went anywhere apart from the crew's population, so the lines of which man belonged to which captain had faded to a blur. The captains thus indiscriminately pulled rank to delegate chores; however, half the men didn't realize we had captains and the other half clearly didn't care. Captain Núñez, whether by humility or some perverse pride, managed to stay among the half that didn't care. He never stood any straighter and largely delegated work to himself.

His insistence on clearing the path in my stead was then no surprise; useful physical labor seemed like his badge of honor. Perhaps he thought it might also slight my pride, taking the harder jobs so I could brood and hate how much better a man he must be. It was a decent plan by any count. What he couldn't yet understand is that I too held social standing in low regard, much less than even he did. So it was no slight to me, who myself rose to Lieutenant from an indifference to doing so, that Núñez performed my lesser tasks. We were both here anyway, stealing the adventure meant for two scouts.

Núñez carved through the brushwood for some additional hours, passing us through miles of thick forest until at last we spotted a small native hut. Sticks and twine made up the roof, while its base and doorway were supported with compact tree trunks and a hard sealant mud. As we walked farther, the forest grew thinner and the grass grew shorter, and at a certain point the trees opened into a path; we now saw a group of huts, the tribal gathering place, bunched together like a town in the forefront of the clearing. However, even in this mass of lodges, the woods maintained an air of emptiness. The natives had dropped their belongings on the ground, almost carelessly it seemed. Our task of assessing the local inhabitants of this La Florida bay had been rendered unsuccessful. Remnants of their daily work were scattered as far as the camp's outskirts in a manner all too thoughtless for any premeditated effort; piece by piece we overturned each tool, not sure of its use yet knowing it was useful. A lot had been left, and all of it had been left in a hurry. We took much less than we could carry.

A fire pit was in the village center (typical indígena practice, from what I'd read). The burnt scent grew even stronger, and at a close glance, we could see how the flames had run their course.

"It's been stamped out," Núñez said.

I knelt overtop the pile, lifting out a piece of charred wood. "That explains why the smoke's gone."

We gaped at the camp for a moment; it didn't take eyes to see that the village was fully deserted.

"All gone," Núñez informed me. His forehead wrinkled with strain and age. "But they didn't leave anything worth a damn."

I chuckled in acknowledgment. "They assumed we were coming?"

Núñez gave a quick nod. "Ships must've scared them."

I responded with a simple grunt, and the two of us rose to leave. The camp had nothing else to offer.

Our first thought was to head back toward the other men, who were beached with the ships a day's walk away. Núñez and I had Governor's orders to return to the expedition before sunrise; but since we were scouting, we decided to search the surrounding streams first. One of these streams flowed slowly toward the bay where our ships had landed. The stream was only a mile from the native camps, so we immediately saw the many additional items that had been left beside it.

A net, an oar, coil, several spears, and a canoe—all lying in the dirt.

"Looks like someone went fishing," I observed.

Núñez smiled and picked up a spear. "It's a wonder they left these," he said. "They're sturdy, and sharp too." He pressed his finger on the edge of the spearhead. With a cut, he quickly pulled back. "Yes," he assured. "These are very good spears."

I might have examined a spear myself, but at that moment I spotted the sickly gray fungus beginning to grow around my feet. The wrapped stockings were damp and unwieldy, and by now I had truly no use for them. I sat in the dirt to unravel them.

"You still don't have boots?" Núñez asked.

I shook my head. "Nobody has a free pair."

Núñez nodded with a hidden smirk, then examined his own boots. Hardly a fray to be seen. Funny, considering his leather was of fool's gold quality and the square shape had grown ever more out of style. Though I admit they were more fashionable than rotting socks. But just as he took pride in his sturdy, clogish clunks, I too was proud of the hastiness which made mine fall apart.

I spent fourteen years in University. That is normally a brow-raising feat, though not within a family like the Castillo-Maldonado. Now, it is not a particularly rich family, nor recognizable, nor noble in any sense bar tax exemption; but being from this hidalgo bunch meant placement in a long line whose careers included living, learning, and leeching off the Universidad de Salamanca since AD 1202. First a custodian, then a gatekeeper, then a secretary, then a secretary's daughter who slept with a professor, then the fruit of that endeavor who was granted an education in economics, followed by more studious un-notables, until finally a father and mother both in love with the field of medicine. The father professed for future doctors and the mother gleaned from his books to nurse frugal students in their second-floor apartamento. They had a son in me. But I didn't much like medicine, or economics, or law, or theology, or even University in general; I did, however, enjoy the humanities enough to live, learn, and leech my own fill for a fourteen-year extended adolescence. So much time wasted, in retrospect, but the thick of that life made it hard to think clearly. I found myself a self-coddling professional student tossed across departments of impracticality and reassurance. Pitiful when measured against the real world. La Universidad had nuggets of beauty, to be sure; I just had to make sure they were unblemished and put back in the correct aisle for the next suckling dote.

My intended course in life? Hopefully not. *Then what in hell was I working towards?* Theoretical questions, but with clear answers. Adventure and exploration were the cures to my insulation. I had to get out.

I never had use for any boots—only sandals. But my father had two pairs which he kept beside the door. I at once began to slip on his newer pair, with the duckbill front and darker leather; however, I caught myself in time, realizing that my abrupt departure was enough of a wound and stealing his better footwear would veer toward the cruel. I slipped them off and fastened on the older ones, which had square fronts just like Núñez's. Not my greatest choice in style, but time was of the essence and I could not dwell. I dropped my parting note on the ground where his boots had been. I wore them in on my walk to purchase a horse.

I cited literacy and basic knowledge of accounting as justification for an officer's role in the expedition. I also offered my new horse. I left from the port of Sanlúcar with the soldiers, nobles, and social deviants who comprised the crew. We reached Cuba in the Fall and the thunderstorms waterlogged my father's boots until they crumbled. Had they been the newer pair, they would have survived.

I tossed my socks aside to let them idle with the other pointless items. After getting up, the dirt was easy to pat off. At least the rest of my outfit was well intact.

Núñez had lost interest in taking pleasure from my plight and was looking around at the scene of tribal departure. His focus soon shifted to the fishing net. It rested halfway into the water, filled with enough dirt to kill an ant colony.

He started shaking out the net, letting the dust fall through until it was nearly empty. Only a few tools, stones, and broken arrow shafts were left. Núñez ripped a large hole in the net, then grabbed a rock from inside; it was muddy, and about the same size as a musket ball.

He came over to me with an open palm.

"What does this seem like to you, Castillo?"

I told him it was just a rock.

Núñez shrugged, unconvinced. He then walked toward the stream and lowered the stone into the water. With his two fingers, he rubbed away at the layer of grime that had collected, and as it cleared, a glint began to reflect off the surface of the object. It was with amazement that I realized the natives had left an actual thing of value... the piece in his hand was more than a simple tool. I excitedly shouted aloud. For a while he and I stared, unable to take our eyes off the glittering metal.

CHAPTER 3

Dulchalchelin

ALVAR NÚÑEZ

La Florida Territory, 1528

The Governor spoke to us in a huddle. "Núñez, if you weren't already Captain, I'd promote you," he said. "Castillo, I'm making you a Captain now too. You men pulled off something incredible today."

Castillo took the news with a smile. "I'm honored..."

I interjected. "Governor, I'd like to go looking for more. If you give me a troop of thirty or so, I'm confident I can discover larger deposits."

The Governor stared me down with his one un-patched eye. "You get right to it, don't you? Alright. I can arrange some horsemen for you, Núñez. Leave at dawn."

"Yes, sir."

My dispatch strapped up and rode in stride behind me. A full week into our endeavor, the excitement of a single gold nugget was keeping our pace inspired.

Miles ridden through the woods, and the muddy ground began to harden.

"You hear that?" someone asked. Everyone turned.

I had heard it, the rustling of leaves deep in the woods. Human figures were the cause.

"Keep your horses quiet," I muttered. "We don't want to miss 'em."

The crew dismounted. We kept moving, anxiously, and the indís, I figured, were moving quickly, quietly, hidden behind the trees; they were all around us, I knew it, and I wanted to catch them.

"They're here," Fray Xuarez said. The monk wasn't much for appearances. Why had the Governor put a monk in this troop?

We all grew quiet again; I listened for a beat against the path, and when it came, I readied for the right moment to end their pursuit.

I turned to my nearest companion. "Alright... Fire."

Andrés Dorantes, a captain in his own right, fired a musket-ball into the native's leg. We heard him cry out in unfamiliar pain.

"Good shot," I said.

The other indígenas gave up their place among the trees, running to the aid of their friend; but if they had ever heard a gun before, they would have known to run in the other direction.

"Wait. Leave them be." I held out my arm. "There's just three, and they don't know what they're doing."

The men obeyed. Those with muskets lowered them. It would have been stupid—not to mention heartless—to finish them off, seeing how frantic they were; but I couldn't let them flee. I needed to maximize the leadership I had been given.

"Try to keep them where they are," I directed. "We don't want them fleeing."

My men grabbed the hunters and shoved them to their knees; there was no strong resistance, thanks mostly to the wounded one. We lifted him over the shoulders of two of the others and moved them close enough that his wrists could be bound to theirs. Then we tied together their open wrists so that the three were an interconnected mass which could transport his wounded load. We got them to their feet. The fourth native we bound by himself.

"Let's take them until we reach another clearing," I said, remounting my horse. "I don't want us getting ambushed again."

The native bundle had trouble moving, but we kept it afloat in the middle of our entourage. We rode a few miles northeast before coming to a place of open grass at which to stop.

"Untie them," I said. "They won't try anything. Maybe we can discover more about the gold and our new territory."

Andrés Dorantes carefully cut their ropes with his blade. The natives wore only thin loincloths, with none of the feathered piercings and smeared paints that most men assumed. The hunters hardly made a movement as their wrists went free; they were much more modest than I had heard.

I reached inside my shirt, pulling out a piece of tied cloth: I untied and unwrapped it, then held out the gold that was inside.

I pointed to my palm. "Have you seen this before?"

They looked up. Beady young eyes watched my words.

The indígena hunters obviously didn't speak a Latin dialect, and there wasn't a sound in their tongue which had any meaning to me. All they could tell was that we were men of power. That much was evident in their buckled posture.

"Where can I find more of this?" My grimy brows furrowed. "You want to say?"

Blank stares. I scoffed, half for show. I had learned enough over the years from more ruthless soldiers to try a few mind games myself. The youngest turned to the others, not quite certain what to do; one of them seemed to be holding his breath.

"No? You don't know?" There was further silence. I rewrapped the gold, somberly stepping back, then I placed it, covered, in my shirt. "It's time to head to their camps," I told the men. "And these hunters are going to be kind enough to lead us there."

We lifted the hunters to their feet, pushed them to the front, and then mounted our horses; instead of using the more open path we had arrived upon, we departed along the natives' hidden trail. They slowly became aware of our intended course. Four indígena faces fell pale with concern over our destination; fearing personal injury, they had no other choice but to comply. My ploy had been a success.

The need for caution vanished, for our new guides kept steady and silent ahead of us. They had learned to obey our few muskets after only one interaction, so it didn't take long to nudge them toward their village. I ordered the crew not to dismount before the hut of the chieftain. This way, as I hoped, we would reach the camp within a few hours, all without another potentially dangerous encounter. Destination reached, time spared, and native compliance; this was a job well done.

This particular La Florida chief, under whom our guides lived, resided in the largest dwelling, where some deerskins covered the ground and the opening was high enough to fit our tallest man. I certainly had no trouble walking through. A feather's quill was pierced through his right ear (finally, the feathers I had heard about), and he had an appearance of wisdom despite his younger features. My guess was he knew not to provoke us.

He rose to greet me with a smile. With a nod hello, I unearthed the cloth from my shirt. Upon seeing the unraveled gold, the chief studied it for a moment before leading me outside to the village campfire. There were tools left about from the day's labor, some from the women and some from the men, but the chief sifted through all of them to lift a single mallet. It had an obvious golden hue, as shining as the piece in my hand... the chief handed it to me.

I didn't know how to ask where we could find more, and that very curiosity caused me to fumble around my words and fingers. Delivering on my promise to the Governor—that I would discover a greater abundance of gold—could grant me further freedoms in leading men on my own. Who knows when a benefit like that might be useful? I simply needed to find a way of communicating my desire to the chieftain.

Pulling from my past experience with foreign locals, who sometimes housed me during the Italian War, I had gathered the fundamentals of speaking across tongues. I subscribed to the belief that motivated demeanor creates meaning almost as well as common language. With purpose, I could point to the golden mallet or the pellet in my hand to portray my message. The chieftain slowly validated these efforts. He led me a few steps toward the village center.

There was an elderly man sitting by the fire and the chief grabbed his attention. They said several things about whatever business, none of which was comprehensible, until the chief finally turned back my way.

"Apalache," he said, then he pointed to the northwest.

I returned to the Governor with my news about Apalache. He was overjoyed to hear it. He immediately convened a small counsel to discuss the best course of action; but instead of including me, the man who had discovered the gold and the vital information of where to find more, he gathered only the monk Fray Xaurez and his favorite captain, Pantoja.

Did he distrust me? Was this why he had sent his monk along in my dispatch? Perhaps the cold arm of bureaucracy had reached into the expedition; my merits were at risk of being undercut.

Whether by personal intent or the convincing word of his counsel, the Governor came to his decision. "I've decided that we will be separating from our ships," he later said to all his captains and officers. "Half the expedition will remain onboard, sailing to Nueva España. The other half will head northwest to Apalache on foot. Go ahead and spread word of this among the men." The Governor imparted some more details, then we disbanded.

I hated the plan to separate; it was rash, too sudden. The plan seemed like something from Hernán Cortés, but without the thought or necessity.

Most of the other expedition men felt similarly displeased, and soon the whole crew was sulking around the bay, waiting for the Governor to change his mind. I reassured them, saying our dilemma would be fixed after I talked with him. But frankly, I was as worried as anyone.

The worst complaint came from a man whose wife was being ordered to head west with the ships. There were still around a dozen women in the expedition (those who hadn't bailed at our supply stop in Cuba some months ago), and all of them wanted to stay with their husbands. The Governor, however, refused to let them venture north; knowing the north would bring added dangers, he required the remaining women to sail westward toward the already-settled ports in Nueva España. The wives didn't like this. For the most part, their husbands were horsemen, and the horsemen were all heading north in search of Apalache. Couples would therefore soon be separated, most likely for an indefinite amount of time. One such cavalier came to me very scatter-brained, convinced his marriage would be destroyed by this sudden separation.

I calmed him, then went to talk things over with the Governor.

The Governor sat on a stretch of grass beneath the shade, with a beard that was always kept short and a head of deep red hair. His hair he kept long to hide a thick black leather strap. This held the patch firmly in front of the Governor's left eye, and he never dared to leave it uncovered. Someone had cut the eye from its socket several years ago.

"Núñez, you know you aren't the first person to come to me today..." He looked at me for a moment and then smiled. "I want to listen, honestly, but nobody has been able to tell me what the real problem is. They just gripe. I can't change anything if the men don't know what they're complaining about."

"I can understand that, Governor," I said. "But I believe I understand what they're complaining about." I hesitated. "I wonder, though, if you really want me to say."

His face creased like a contemplative hound. "Don't toy with me, Núñez. Just say it."

I gave a slight nod. "Well, their main concern is that if we separate from the ships, then we will also be leaving the supplies. The ships will be stocked full with as much as they want, but anyone riding north won't have anything except what can be carried; we'll have to leave the rafts, the barrels, and most of the food..."

"There's food in the wild." The Governor grinned. "Real men don't need a pack full of ship-biscuit hanging from their backs when there's enough out there to hunt."

He stared at me with keen confidence, and I realized he wasn't about to be convinced. I stood straighter. "Governor, if we do this, then we're going north without security. None of the men think it's wise, and I happen to agree. I don't know what else to say."

"Hmph..." He gave a grunt. "Núñez, I assume you've heard that I too will not be remaining with the ships?"

"Yes, I heard," I said. He had told me and the other captains as much only hours prior.

"Well, you've even said yourself that the land is a much riskier route to take—and it is, by all means." The Governor gazed at the five vessels beached with our supplies. "I'm not leading those ships. Whatever dangerous fate I'm putting on the men, I'm putting on myself as well." The Governor slowly rose, still facing the water. "You've got your reasons for concern, and I understand that. But if you really think it's such a foolish plan, then I'll honor that opinion: I won't make you go north with us. You're a fine captain, and despite your stubbornness, I think you'd do a good job of leading the fleet."

My face immediately dropped. The Governor had me cornered. I shook my head in reply.

"This is about more than my own safety," I said. "My concerns are serious, Governor."

"As is my offer," he said, smiling. "I want you to take the ships to Nueva España. You think you can handle that, Captain?"

I shook my head again, my complexion red. "No, I'm as much obliged to stay with the expedition as you are. It would ruin me to be absent while you all went north."

The Governor let out a jolting chuckle. "But all those rafts and barrels are sailing for the ports," he said. "Is current expedition property not as important as future property?"

In my mind, I cursed him. He rightly knew that a man of my skill should not be consigned to guiding barrels to a port. Outwardly, I managed a rough sigh and a dissenting head-shake.

"You'll have to find someone else to watch the ships," I said. "I'm not abandoning this expedition's true purpose."

The Governor became grim, but finally let out a "fair enough," then told me to be prepared for our trek north. His plans were already well underway.

Three hundred of us agreed to make the journey inland. Every last captain, officer, and monk refused to remain with the ships. A nobleman, Caravallo, was eventually chosen to lead the fleet across the gulf. He was level-headed, charismatic, and a little bit cowardly: the perfect man to abandon the crew's true purpose. The fleet was to head due west for a port near the end of the Pánuco River in Nueva España, only circling back if we had not arrived by winter. The landlocked horsemen cried for their wives, and the wives, fearing for their husbands' lives, grappled with the prospect of finding new men.

Our first job was to sort our smaller cut of the supplies. There were personal items, like clothes and knives, swords, muskets, bibles and rosary beads—but we did not own much else. None of us would be riding horses. Yes, even the horsemen. The relative few steeds left for us would have to carry our rations and water sacks on their backs; we did not have the strength to do it ourselves. Each man received a two-pound ration of biscuit and salted ham that was sure to last no more than a week at best. From then on, our food would be whatever we could catch. And what would the horses eat?

Fifteen days of trekking passed; we didn't encounter a single native. It convinced me that most of La Florida was abandoned, save for the occasional cluster. It was not until the sixteenth day that we came across the first group living in this northern region.

The tribe, somehow aware of our approach, decided to meet us outside their village before we arrived. Instead of bows and arrows, they carried flutes made from reeds, playing so loudly that I heard them miles away. Soon enough I saw them proceeding as a parade behind their chieftain, a man sitting on the shoulders of two younger huntsmen. It was akin to a Biblical kingdom. Maybe Babylon or Nineveh, I don't know. His age, however, was hidden behind a thick smear of dye and the deerskin which covered his back; he did not come off his human pedestal until the tribe had finished their melody. As he approached, the facial contours behind his painted exterior became more visible.

The Governor stated our business simply with the word *Apalache*; it was too much to try any other form of communication. Regardless, the chieftain made it clear that he was not Apalache, but was "Dulchalchelin." The entire region shared his name and the tribe considered it sacred. At least that's what I gathered.

It took an hour for Chief Dulchalchelin and the Governor to come to an understanding, yet when they did, our two sides reached a fair agreement. Dulchalchelin would lead us northwest, to Apalache, but only on the condition that his vengeance on their tribe would not be hindered. The Apalache had ambushed the Dulchalchelin years before, and he wanted nothing more than a raid of his own. The gold could be ours for all he cared. Again, that's at least what I gathered.

We walked into the night. Chief Dulchalchelin took his tribe across the river that was in our path, promising to wait for us until we crossed it ourselves. There weren't enough of his canoes to fit our horses and supplies, so we would have to manage another way. The Governor decided we should rest and attempt to cross in daylight.

Many of the men refused to sleep that night, bothered that we were waiting until morning.

The horseman Juan Velázquez muttered to his friend. "The last river didn't take us too long," he said, staring ahead. "Don't see why we should take a whole day when we could cross it in an hour on horseback."

"But this one has a current," the other man said. "It's too strong to risk the supplies."

Juan Velázquez shrugged. "It's not going to make too much of a difference if one man goes out alone."

I wondered to myself if he was the same Juan Velázquez my wife always spoke of.

The other man looked at Juan, muttering something, but soon I stopped listening. It was late and I was tired. A captain who is not alert in the daylight can never lead.

I awoke to the sound of a horse drowning in the river. When it neighed, like a wild beast, a man clutched its neck, beginning to drag it purposelessly beneath the water. The man had lost his grip, the reins slipped, and he was struck dumb with fear, pressed beneath his horse; he tried desperately to catch a breath, but he couldn't get out; he was underneath; he pulled its mane harder and the horse cried out in all the more pain. The horse didn't want to die, but the man was caught, given no other options. There wasn't any other way to breathe; yet while his breath slowly ran out, a steady stream pumped into the lungs of his steed; it choked, crying no longer. Soon the horse's weight fell under, and the dead man beneath it was carried off by the rushing current. It was a miserable sight to wake up to.

The crew debated eating the drowned horse. One group figured they should get ahead of the dwindling rations, so they went ahead with the idea. The horse had been lying next to Juan's body in a place where the current slowed, and the men were hungry enough to pull it from the water. I refused to eat its meat, however well cooked, and I soon discovered how wise my choice had been: their dysentery set in two days later. Infection tore their intestines, turning waste to a mess of blood and saliva to a dark, cloudy brown. Piles along the trail-side gave off an enclosing scent; I walked with my head hung low, waiting for the inevitable deaths of those ruined by a rancid meal. Nineteen were lost by the end of a trying month. They were buried along the trail, laid beneath the evidence of what had befallen them. Our expedition began to get a lot quieter.

Summer rapidly approached, and the Dulchalchelin walked leagues ahead. One unusually humid afternoon, however, I spotted them coming back towards us. Chief Dulchalchelin's subordinates were far too worn to carry him now; besides, the procession had served only as an introduction. The Chief walked past the Governor, and with a single glance it was clear: the Dulchalchelin were returning home. Heat, exhaustion, and sickness were affecting them just as heavily.

The Governor simmered, with a red face and an angry eye. He avoided the crew's questions to stand by himself for some minutes, collecting his emotions and staving off an outburst.

We stalled our progress to camp for the night. Tall, sturdy trees surrounded us. It was a testament to the severity of the winter's storms that they were no longer overhead but on the ground. Bay oaks and junipers made our bed, and shredded leaves covered the fallen trunks like deceptive blankets.

Castillo boyishly laid his bedroll (a supply sack and a quilt) near the inspector Solis, who had quickly fallen asleep. Neither Castillo nor I drifted off so easily; he turned to face me, regretfully.

"When we found the gold, I was ecstatic," he said. "Are you still feeling the excitement, Núñez?"

"No, I don't know if I ever felt it quite like you did," I said. "It was only a pellet." When talking to Castillo, you almost had to humor him. He knew how to converse, but he wasn't as skilled with the *when* or the *with whom*.

"Do you not want to be wealthy?" he asked.

"If I need to, yes," I said, rolling onto my side. "I'm just not yet sure what gold can actually do in La Florida. Where can my money go in a place that isn't even established?"

Castillo's eyes had darkened since I met him. His already slender frame had lost its child's chub. His hands, though, were still uncalloused. "True. Even if you were rich, you'd still have to listen to the Governor."

I laughed. "Yes, and he'd probably run that wealth back into the ground with his mindless decisions."

Castillo nodded. He picked up a twig from under his back and tossed it aside. "What do you think the Governor's going to do now that Dulchalchelin's gone?"

"He'll panic," I said. "But just because our guides have left, it doesn't mean Apalache is any farther away. I'll make sure he stays on course."

Castillo smiled. "Ah, so you think Apalache is close? The men are dropping quickly, and who knows how much longer we'll hold together."

"We'll last," I said. "There's damp ground under these logs, which means a stream or lake must be close. Odds are there are people living nearby, and they might be the Apalache."

Castillo finally reclined from his upright posture. "I see. So, if the Governor listens to you, we'll soon be resting in a nearby village, convincing them to give us some food."

"No, you've got it all wrong," I said, turning fully onto my back. "Even if the nearest tribe is weaker than what the Apalache are said to be, our fate would be in their hands. With or without the Dulchalchelin's support, we need to take advantage of our obscured position. I'm going to launch an ambush."

His brow shot up. "You are?"

"Yes. The Governor can join me if he likes," I said. "I'm not letting the opportunity slip away; we need a home base, and there's no better spot than right above a gold deposit."

Castillo's face dropped, and I could see the revulsion of his sheltered innocence. He knew nothing.

War had taught me time and again that orchestrating a decisive victory can forever change a man's status. It can also ward off unforeseen calamity. If I was going to be known for anything, it would be the raid of Apalache.

CHAPTER 4

Raiding Apalache

ALONSO DEL CASTILLO

Apalache, North of Tampa Bay, Summer of 1528

Alvar Núñez brought over the carpenter, guiding him by the shirt collar to where the older Captain Pantoja was standing.

"Here he is," Núñez said. "This is Fernández, the Portuguese carpenter. He can build us the wheelbarrow, and we can take the corpses further outside the village, dig the hole, and bury them."

"No," said Pantoja. "There's no need."

"Don't be ridiculous. You can't just leave her there." Núñez stared somberly at the young woman, face down in the dirt.

"She doesn't need a burial, and the rest of them don't either." Pantoja scowled. "The bitch gave me sores; they've been showing up on all the other men too."

There were indeed a few by his lips.

"But, Captain, what do you think the Friar will say?" Núñez matched the bluntness of the crotchety man a decade his senior. "You think he'll like having all these bodies go without a Christian burial?"

"Huph. Bury the indís? Next, you'll marry 'em," Pantoja mumbled.

"Watch yourself. I'm not the one who raped half the village." Núñez gazed with simmering anger. "If they're not good enough to bury, then they're not worth getting sores over."

Pantoja ignored him. "Fray Xuarez!" he shouted at the monk who was sitting not far from me. "D'you mind if these indís go without a ceremony?"

My head was rested against a log, but I listened in with a distant heart. Something similar could be said of the Friar's slumped posture. Pantoja's cocky face dropped more and more the longer Fray Xuarez sat silent, as if the words hadn't reached his ears.

The silver-haired captain turned instead to the Portuguese carpenter. "Well, Fernández or whatsername, you heard him as well as I did. Head on back to what you were doing."

"No, no, hold on," Núñez grabbed the carpenter before he could walk off. "Fernández, stay right here awhile. We're still going to need you."

"Alright, Captain, yes," Fernández said. His Castilian wasn't very good, though he sure said "yes" and "captain."

Núñez looked at Fray Xuarez, seeking a solution, but the head monk was motionless. So he turned my way in desperation. "Castillo, can you talk some sense into the Friar? He takes well to sensitivity."

Sensitivity? Me? And to ask me, another captain... how rude. But like I said, I never much cared for power dynamics; so, I slumped up from my rest, told him "sure thing," and walked a few paces over to the Friar.

"Fray, you want to talk?" I said. "You're acting off-color."

He sighed. His green drapes hung low. They fitted him about as well as the priesthood. "Yes, we can talk; but I'm not getting up."

I stood between him and the view of Núñez and Pantoja. They were still bickering.

"Why not?" I asked.

"It's that girl. Yesterday, she was on everybody's mind, moved from hut to hut, and yet now... well, I've never seen someone lose favor so quickly." He glanced up at me. "And I'm supposed to be preaching, you know. I can't convert a tribe when they're all dead."

I realized now what Núñez meant by sensitivity. The Friar needed someone without abundant bloodlust—or weaponized general lust—to listen.

"You can't beat yourself up about it, Fray; those men were going to take retribution regardless. Sex with consequence is a capital offense in their eyes."

Strange it was, talking morals with a monk.

"Ah, but it's not just that." Fray Xuarez grew antsy. "The expedition has other purposes considered more important than the Gospel: I get that. But the raid took over so completely, you see, that almost as quick as we saw the indís, they're gone, and I couldn't get a word about salvation in edgewise. It's not how the Church operates."

Perhaps Fray Xuarez had been stuck in seminary during the Inquisition. Us Catholics (if I could consider myself one) were for similar reasons not too popular with the Jews back in Salamanca. Or they had been in Salamanca that is.

He did make a strong point about the brevity of our friendliness in Apalache, however. It was certainly a gross village. Toppled trees, muddy ground, and thatched, ugly huts would make any resident depressed. But it's not like our response to the place helped matters. Núñez's ambush took hold, left his guidance, and grew into a massacre. Apalache became our hell-hole. Fray Xuarez himself was now a monument to it; a ratty head of hair met his tired, dirt-smeared face.

We had entered with the emoted version of "where's the gold?" Their answer: no gold. "You're lying." It's the truth, they said. They didn't say it all too nicely. They were crabby people—like I said, depressed from the landscape—and to be honest, after having trekked for weeks through the very same, I felt rather crabby myself. I wouldn't have minded hitting one or two of them.

The Governor. Teetering between collapse and inspiration. "Núñez, we're moving forward with your plan. Alright, men, toss this place apart. Let's find the gold."

At first, I felt no qualms. Killing has never sat well with me, but I was grateful to punch the indígena hunter who had given me a sideways glance. My virgin fist was satisfied. But then the adrenaline of some men rose to the point of stabbing and shooting; local resistance posed no dire threat in return.

Lots of indígenas died in a seven days' raid. I kept my head and hands away from the horrid acts around me. Núñez had meant to displace the potentially hostile tribe, but many Spaniards were executing his initial plan beyond all reason. The Apalache tribe had been described as brutal by Chief Dulchalchelin; no tribe, however, deserved their fate. Were all of us slaughtering indís and forcing ourselves on women? No. But it only takes a few to unleash mass destruction to its fullest. During the raid, there were certainly more than a few who did.

I occupied myself with menial auxiliary tasks. When the University is your Church, you adhere to pacifism above the Lord. I remained steadfast enough to turn my cheek the other way. The answer as to what motivated the most violent men stayed elusive, and it plagued me.

The Governor. "Where's the gold?" The men were frantic. "We looked everywhere!" Men began to burn the huts after each search.

The Governor was slow to respond; he had finally teetered the way of collapse, made ill from gold-lost heartache. Instead, Núñez mustered the strength to address them. "No, we need those! We're sleeping in those now!"

By then half the village was burned. We didn't know what to do with the male corpses; they were lying outside our new huts. Restlessness truly took over. The old indí women ran off with their young sons and daughters, afraid that the boys would soon be killed and the girls would soon flower into the arms of a Castilian ruffian. A legitimate concern. Not too many of the indígena women were surviving the wrath of the sore-laden gentlemen; or, if they were, their quality of life had severe limitations. There grew an odd orchestra of crying around the huts. Women grieved their stolen bodies as deceased husbands were scattered by men grieving lost enchantment and derailed purpose. The limb-littered ground and rotting stench overwhelmed so heavily that now two captains were discussing a wheelbarrow to clean the clutter, while a priest turned to a secular intellectual for his spiritual guidance.

"Get up there, Fray Xuarez!" I said with a forceful whisper. "Don't you know that having God's representative sit aside is wrecking us? Forget conversion! We're in need of you, so get up and clean us from this mess of self-destruction and sin in which we wallow." I looked him straight in the eyes. "Do Christ's bidding."

Did I believe in the concept of sin? No, but I disliked how these terrible things made me feel. And Jesus? Well, he had lived I suppose.

Fray Xuarez reeled at my words. Round his head they seemed to swirl until he slowly gained his sense and arose. "All right," he said. "I will save this."

You will? Not your God? But alas, I was pleased.

"Ah, Fray!" Captain Pantoja's gray beard stretched. "Glad you got up."

"Pantoja." Fray Xuarez sneered. "Maybe you didn't notice the dead piles already building high; but since you couldn't restrain yourself in stabbing this girl, perhaps you could help us cart her off to a burial. This camp needs to be purged."

Pantoja's grin dropped to a frown. Núñez sighed in relief.

"Carpenter!" Fray Xuarez turned to the man. "You and some men are going to spend the next two days building a barrow from all this fallen wood. We're going to have a ceremony for these unsaved souls."

"Alright, priest, yes," said the Portuguese Fernández.

The carpenter went straight to work, and the captains—one distressed by his culpability and the other begrudgingly accepting his confines—went their separate ways.

I had spent my whole life hating the Church as an institution of remarkable sway and discord. I believed I walked in circles of enlightened people in a higher institution, one promoting curiosity and true advancement; now, after souring to the University and coming to a place in which it could not hold footing, I saw the common denominator among foolish men. For the first time in my life I thanked the Church, glad for its granting a well-meaning oaf the authority to make chaos seem more orderly.

Burying the natives gave us the idea to dig for gold. If it was not in the huts, then there should have been an explanation for its absence. Perhaps the Apalache didn't value it; they must never have mined for the gold. It must still be under the ground, right?

It wasn't.

"Christ, I could use a drink," Núñez said to me. But we had run out. We left all the rum, to be more precise, with the ships that were probably in Nueva España by now. Some men had packed along a bottle or two, but everyone knows how short that amount lasts, especially for the type of man who would even worry about bringing rum in the first place. But at a moment like this, we truly needed it. I could have benefited from some myself.

Núñez's grand vision had burst into existence and descended into debauched meaninglessness. The military man, the man of strategy, was forlorn to see his pursuit end without accomplishment. The home base he had claimed was not viable. I left him to his brooding.

What's a man in the presence of desperation to do in the absence of drink? Well, for a small few, they bend a knee to pray. Cry for help and the like. For those similar to me, we internalize the struggles for later digestion: the least abrasive response, I would say. Yet, for the larger lot, there's always women. At least, that is, until the sores have spread to a point where no one is comfortable with an Apalache woman. And since the burial hole had already been made and filled, and the men did not want to dig another one, the surviving women were released rather than killed. How compassionate.

So here I stood in a charred camp filled solely with uncomfortable, unhappy men waiting for... What? The Governor?

Yes, for the Governor.

Just because he didn't feel well?

Yes, exactly. His condition had worsened.

Alright, fine by me. But only because a sick leader cannot, obviously, be carried by his couple hundred men on their departure. No, that would be improper. He must remain tucked away and coddled in privacy as long as the sickness incapacitates him. A visibly weak leader would ruin morale. The men wouldn't, of course, take the sickness for what it is, a separate measure entirely from leadership. The two qualities would, without a doubt, be correlated irreparably. The men would never see their Governor the same way again. So alas, they must remain for his sanctity's sake in the Apalache hell-hole until a full recovery is made.

Thirty days passed in total.

The Governor emerged, hunched and battered. He smelled awful. He must have truly been in terrible shape for his closest aides to have now said, "What a recovery! Let's get him to his feet." Despite my prior frustrations, I actually did question whether we in the crew would see our Governor the same way again. The sight certainly was not a morale booster.

Our feet were motivated, though.

The Governor's first action was to address the departure at a meeting of officers. "It is vital," he said, "that we leave at dawn tomorrow. The men have been begging it, and the time has arrived. But as things stand, we know only one potential destination. Apalache has until this point been our guiding beacon; it's taken us a while to get over the disappointment it's caused." *Yes, but you have taken longer than anyone, Governor.* "There is a new option, however. The Comptroller's whore told him about a village called Aute sitting a few leagues off from here. Enriquez, tell us about it."

Comptroller Enriquez was bright, good-looking, and our finest surviving horseman. "Sure thing," he said. "It's supposedly pretty viable. Not loaded with gold or anything, like we were told about Apalache. The opportunity there, in Aute, is that the people know how to grow food. Same barren ground, but they've managed to farm."

"So this means we'll be eating?" The Governor asked, much like a litigator, knowing full well the answer and seeking it only for display to others.

"Yes, it does," said the Comptroller. "I was told to just follow the river toward the gulf. Once we have eyes on the coast, we take it about two leagues Northwest before going another two due North. We could camp right on the gulf."

"That we could. Aute would only be a day's trip away." The Governor nodded exaggeratedly, compensating for his weakness. His eye patch remained stationary. "So, men, we have that option. And seeing as it's been thirty days and no one else has presented another one, we're taking it."

I had no qualms. I was ready to leave.

"We leave at dawn to follow the Aute river."

The river, which felt more like a stream in its slow solitude, ran supposedly through the apex of Aute and into the gulf. Not a wind blew in relief from the humidity, and instead the murky air crept its way farther from the water until the riverbank felt as dense as a swamp. There were no mountains in La Florida to freshen a river's supply; so instead of providing a lifeline, it ran through the country like the spine of a parasite, a cesspool. I followed this river with the rest of the expedition, my feet bruised and bloody, until at last I was within a half day's distance from the Aute gulf-side.

No man had eaten more than a handful in the last few days; my bones felt shot to the brink of collapse, and the hunger was maddening. The rumored crops became more tempting. "Ride ahead to the village," the Governor said to the horsemen. "Do whatever you can to bring back food." So Comptroller Enriquez led the other cavaliers to relieve Aute of its resources. He returned two days later to our newly-set camp, severely worn, his knees on the verge of buckling.

"The tribe refused to feed us," he said. "We didn't want to use force, but they wouldn't take the hint. Their stores were full of maize—we took all they had."

The maize was in sacks, tied to the horses' saddles.

"Thank God!" I exclaimed. Credit where credit's due? Cultural habit, more like.

That first meal might have been one of life's best. Simultaneously juicy and hearty, the maize could be felt from my mouth to my gut, and it made me glad. But the supply seemed to dwindle as fast as an hourglass; five or six meals later, there was not even enough to feed the horses.

What a plight we were in! Where to go next? When? How do we get there when we don't know where it is? Though an entire ocean lay in front of me, I was trapped on this stretch of land without any sustenance or peace of mind. I wanted to flee so desperately, to find a way out.

Others were in fact fleeing, including the very horsemen that had raided Aute. They mounted a steed in whatever direction they saw fit, inspired by hunger and selfish ambition. Seeing them abandon camp somehow deterred my own escapist leanings; I first envied them, then worried for them, then despised them as cowards. I would not become one.

At last the Comptroller could take it no longer, and he, a horse lover, proposed that we all eat the remaining stallions. "They are dying," he said. "If we're hungry, think of how little they have eaten... they can't even carry our bundles any longer. What is the point of giving them food if they starve anyway? We need to cook them before they waste."

No one had an objection to this plan. No one had the strength to object. Thus, every chosen three days, the weakest horse was killed and rationed among the crew; when the rubbery meat was put before us, the act of a meal became considerably more hesitant and a lot less enjoyable. It did, however, serve us better than the small fodder in the woods. I, like everyone, needed to relish in these meals. A beggar cannot choose, even if he does not think himself a beggar.

"Can't we grow more of that maize?" one man asked.

"No, we killed the farmers, remember," answered another.

Fire had been lit below us. Like the maize, the horses were very limited—less than thirty. Though our strength was somewhat restored, it would again dwindle; with each restoration would come another retreat. Was I to die amidst a wasteland of forest and festered swamps?

The Governor must have thought similarly. Mental strain edged the contours of his face. Light brown soil filled his crevices, caking him in the war paint of a broken man. His sickness had been beat, willed out by sheer stubbornness against failure; his hopes, though, were no longer excited. He addressed a gathering of the whole crew.

"Our only option is the sea," the Governor said. Unlike his other recent proposals, this was not announced as a suggestion. "The sooner we can set out, the longer our lives will last." He was haggard, but deadly serious.

So sailing away it would be. But the ships we needed were long gone (Any wonder who approved that plan, Governor?). The crew's westward half wouldn't have known to come back for us so soon; that is, assuming they had any actual intention to do so. If we ever hoped to cross the sea, then we needed more than the simple rafts or canoes; entire functioning vessels were necessary to sail the rough waters of a gulf. We needed to build these from scratch. No outlines, no tools, and no conventional materials. Our diminished endurance aside, the thought frightened even the bravest of us.

Everything found in the forests became a substitute to a necessity. From our limited understanding (as none of us remaining were shipbuilders by trade, though many had lived in port towns), we knew oakum and tackling could construct the frames. We had neither these items nor the tools to craft them together. The company, then, wisely began to burn our metals to be reformed into the other required tools. Bellows were first made out of deerskin (what little we could hunt) in the hopes that they could maintain a hot fire, while at the same time, wooden vents were added to let the smoke rise out. Spurs, crossbows, stirrups, matchlock handles, and necklaces became ferrous bars, malleable enough to make into a saw or hatchet.

"I don't want to burn this," Andrés Dorantes despaired. "It was my father's." We shamed him until he contributed.

The horses became useful for more than meat; the skin of their dead legs was tanned into sacks for storing water; their tails and manes became rope and tackle. Other men found use from the simplest materials—Teodoro, a Greek expatriate, splintered his hand against a pine tree, and in his frustration noticed that the bark's brown sap could be used as a caulking resin. The Portuguese Fernández, our savant carpenter, thus decided to tar the boat beams together with that very same sap.

"Don't eat the palmetto fronds," our camp manager Sotomayor announced. "Fernández says they're fibrous enough to tie off these beams in case the water breaks through." Everyone complied with the request, and the palmetto husks were brought to the carpenter in large supply.

Apart from the pine trees, not many species lined the forests but the juníperos; I went out daily to chop them so that our crew would be able to craft oars. This was my work for the entirety of our shipbuilding effort.

Each juniper tree was fully coated in thick leaves which stemmed from weak, bendable branches, and a thick trunk that held it all together. It took a great deal to hack through the green before the axe (made from the old matchlock handles) cut into the bark. Bright berries adorned the dense needles, which sat at eye level as I worked; as days passed, I had an urge to eat them, but the company learned months ago that the junípero's coniferous fruit was poisonous when uncooked. Some Spaniards from Aragón had supposedly seen the berries used in spices, but they never figured that their casual snacking would cause illness; they learned the hard way not to eat them, yet I now felt so hungry that the lesson was difficult to bring to mind. The combination of sparse horse meat and endless wood-chopping was thinning my body, but leaving a dense layer of muscle in return. Because of it, I managed to withstand the temptation long enough for a next ration. I could bring the junípero berries back to be cooked and enjoyed by all.

We finished building all five vessels in September, two days after the last horse had been slaughtered. Each ran ten meters long at most. They resembled an exiled convict's last attempt back home. They appeared as worthily sewn together as makeshift vessels could be, but they were far from inviting.

The company hurried to load its supplies before our strength wore out. We stocked the clothing bundles, the oars (I was quite proud of them), the horse and deerskin sacks of boiled water, and whatever palmettos remained to be eaten. No space had to be made for animals, none for ammunition; now that our matchlock handles had been cast into iron tools, the muskets too had no place on our jagged deck. Instead, we made room for our mallets, nails, and blunt axes.

Many gave up their shirts to be sewn into sails; I was among them. I had begun to feel incredible worth in the crew-wide effort, and the shirt-sail appeared to be its culmination. In a different vein, to see it blowing in the breeze churned my stomach. Our old ships bore the colors of the imperial flag and the stoic black eagle. These thick sails were nothing but the stains of the earth.

At noon, the Governor called together the captains and expedition officers to detail our departure. He stood well above us, having completely overcome his sickened slant.

"Two men will take charge of each ship," he said. "That's ten fleet captains total, with one pilot per pair. Our original sea navigators may be far ahead of us, but I've chosen our five best water-men to be pilots. Their only job is to gear the boat westward." The Governor pointed them out: five fishermen and port-rats whom none of us knew. "There are two hundred forty men to split between these ships—we captains alone must remain responsible for their lives. *You* must usher your men to Nueva España, is that clear?" His bloodshot eye scanned our faces. *Yes, Governor*, a few assented. "The first ship's going to hold forty-nine," he continued. "I will be in control; assisting alongside me will be Captain Pantoja."

No surprise there. He probably picked the best of the bunch to row for them, too.

"Two more ships are going to have forty-nine passengers each: one under the joint command of Captain Alvar Núñez and Inspector Solis. The other is under the guidance of yourself, Comptroller Enriquez, with the help of Fray Xuarez."

A hundred and forty-seven men accounted for. The Governor beamed at the lovable horseman and doting priest, while my favorite hard-boiled egg, Núñez, and his rather meek new counterpart, the Inspector, nodded in confirmation. The Governor turned to address our other half.

"Forty-eight more will be leaving with Dorantes and del Castillo," he continued. "Mind the sail on your ship; it's the most tattered."

I quickly interrupted. "Which Dorantes do you mean, Governor?"

"'Which Dorantes?'" He sounded annoyed. "There's another Dorantes?"

Yes, there was. Andrés and his little brother Diego, who had just been made a lieutenant, were both present at the meeting. They even brought a Moroccan slave, if you wanted to count a third. But "Yes, Governor, they're both present," was all I offered in explanation.

"Alright, well I'm obviously referring to the one we've called 'Captain' for over a year now. Think, Castillo." He gave me a sore eye and then turned to Andrés. "Tell me your name again."

"Andrés," said the elder Dorantes. He masked his frustration at being so misremembered.

"Yes, Andrés, thanks," replied the Governor. "You and Castillo have the fourth boat."

Captain Dorantes looked at me and so I nodded. He returned a nod.

The Governor straightened his back. "Okay, the last ship is the smallest. Forty-seven men under captains Téllez and Peñalosa. There may be slight variations, but I believe that accommodates everyone." He slowly turned to face the water. His mood became heavier. "It's calm out there," he said. "There's hardly a wave in the gulf today. Nevertheless, I don't want to see anybody get more than a league away from the coastline." He faced us once more. "At any point, if you're too far out, have your men steer back before you even think about moving forward. The other ships can't keep track of you. Don't wait up, and don't get caught behind... we'll all be meeting in Nueva España sometime fairly soon."

He smiled warmly, which tensed his red beard.

Heading to my separate boat, I called out for my assigned men to board. I stepped on after Andrés—his brother and their Morisco slave followed me; after only a moment, the deck was filled to its saturation. Our port-rat pilot lifted the anchor so we could float off, our deck bobbing a mere foot above the water's surface. A base of simple rods tied with tight fronds held us in the sea, and the water sloshed around unpredictably. Our situation on land had been precarious, but the gulf's unknowable trials frightened me even more. The expedition's purpose seemed to be fully derailed. Were we sailing toward Spanish settlements to regroup or to give up? Without the mission of claiming La Florida, avoidable dangers felt all the more worthless. This was the first time I regretted putting on my father's old boots to join the Florida fleet.

CHAPTER 5

Hernán

———

THE GOVERNOR

The Gulf, October 1528

His face haunted me. It had been seven years since I last saw him, but his thin smile was imprinted in my thoughts. On the day when he visited me in my Nueva España cell, his smile stretched a little wider than usual. I was his captive. Hernando Cortés had ruined my life.

The pain in my throat was the same now, on this raft, as it had been in that earthen cell. The feeling was a continual choke, but not as forgiving; it took great lengths to bear, enough that I had not slept in days and did not plan to anytime soon.

Our deerskin flasks were rot. The water inside slowly poisoned any man who drank it, hastening his emaciation. "No more," I said, and told the crew to throw our flasks over; but it took bloodied coughing for them to listen. Even then, some continued to sneak seawater in scoopfuls.

They'd probably be drinking their urine if there was a container to hold it; instead, they managed to keep a shred of dignity by pissing over the sides. Their hands were clean, for now.

Pantoja, my assisting older captain, preferred to recline against the hand-made mast, stretching out his legs to the middle of the deck. Like the flasks, his skin appeared rotted by the gulf sun. "Do you think it'd be smart to take another swig yet?" he asked, hoping to risk it.

"I wouldn't," I said. But Pantoja drank anyway. I bit my lip in frustration at his blatant disregard.

Relief from thirst only came after five days, when the sky finally decided to loosen its rain and thunder; I caught the pellets with my mouth and hands, but the sheer force of the winds often made it difficult. As if to spite me, the black storm-waves became rough and unpredictable. We needed food, but we had drifted far from the coast, and the tide's height made it impossible to even spot it. The same storm barrage that quenched our thirst was crippling us. My eye fixated on the shore as the storm softened.

"We have to get to land today," Captain Pantoja said. "Another storm will kill us."

I nodded. "That's where we're headed."

"True, but at an angle," he said. "We'll get there faster if we stop slanting westward." Pantoja was a stern relic in contrast to the cold air which blew atop the water's surface.

I grunted, considering, but then I remembered the in-line raft sailing much too far from the coast. It was one of ours, though I didn't know which.

"That raft up ahead," I said. "I've been trying to keep it from drifting all the way out to sea. If we go due north, we'll lose sight of it."

"Are you a guardian angel now?" Pantoja playfully grinned. "Remember what you told the others, Governor." His point was strong. I was acting against what I had advised the captains, watching out for a ship beside my own. But I did not enjoy hearing it from my inferior.

"Hmph. Well, it's on you when they die, Pantoja, if that makes you any happier." He chuckled, and I turned to the skipper. "Don't worry too much about keeping the western slant anymore. We have to get to shore a bit sooner than I'd hoped." The skipper complied, directing the oarsmen (a third of our men, alternating) to steer toward the northern coast.

I sat in reflection as they rowed. My thoughts returned to Hernando Cortés, how not only his face, but also his words haunted me...

Seven years ago, he entered my cell. He had an air about him that immediately made itself known. He examined the ground, looking at first as if he would remain standing; but instead, he stooped to my level. His legs thudded against the dirt, and he embraced his new surroundings.

"What brings you in here, Hernán?" I asked from my place on the floor. He hated being called Hernán. His smile remained, however.

"Something very important brings me here, soldier," he said. Hernán shifted into position, getting comfortable. He took off his convex-rimmed metal helmet and placed it on the dirt. "I spoke with Rodrigo yesterday. What was he, your third in command?" Hernán waited for me to answer, but I wouldn't give him the satisfaction, as he could well have guessed. He moved on, delighted. "Your old comrade says the Throne is thinking of sending another troop after me. Can you believe that? After how it went last time, when you were at the helm, I might have thought they would leave me be. It's needless bloodshed, and a huge political headache."

I did not fear him. "You sure get quite the ego trip from political headaches, Hernán."

"Mmm, perhaps," he said, as if I was some friend with whom he discussed philosophy. "But this time, it won't be the same. I plan to develop it a little differently."

"How so?" I asked, leaning straighter against the unfurnished wall.

"That's what I came to you for," Hernán said. "You're going to help me."

I was stunned, but I didn't show it. I kept calm.

He continued. "The new fodder they're sending must assume you weren't successful in bringing me in... otherwise, I'd be dead. They're probably wondering where you are, which is the very reason I've left you with these indís. I can't give them the impression that I'm holding you, or else it'll go the same way it did with you. I'm trying to avoid that. I don't need more Iberian blood on my hands, or pressure from the King... or to humiliate another general by stealing the loyalty of his men. My army is full."

Hernán was of course referring to the pain he had caused me in dismantling my troop from the inside. As I faced greater losses against him, he increased the prospects of joining his rank, until he finally crushed any hope of my mission to bring him in succeeding. Those men who were disloyal to me he absorbed, those loyal he imprisoned, and those who were outspoken antagonists he killed.

"How come you didn't just kill me?" I asked. "It would have solved your problems just as easily."

Hernán chuckled. "To be frank, I did give orders to kill you if you ever ran away. It seems like you've had the sense to stay put, though." He was certainly correct in that I hadn't tried running away; my few remaining friends were all imprisoned elsewhere, and there was no chance I'd be able to convince someone to guide me to safety.

I cleared my throat. "What can I say... this cell's pretty comfortable compared to the place in hell they've marked for you."

He happily ignored me and continued. "The indís you're staying with, they are a tribe who have been helping me fight the Aztecas. They've been the best help, actually, because they're the strongest allies I managed to rope in." Hernán's smile started to drop a little. "Most of the other tribes were easy to convince: they're angry with the Aztecas for abusing their power. But this tribe, the one who's been taking care of you, envies them more so as competition. I've had to promise them this and that in exchange for help with the war, and it so far has caused me no trouble. But now, I'm no longer in need of help with fighting my battles; the Aztecas are so sick that I don't even have to attack them. They keep dying, and all I need to do is wait."

His successes cut at my core. "So, what do you have planned for these Azteca imitators?" I said.

"Patience," Hernán said. He paused for a moment, undoubtedly to drive me mad. "Your hosts are strong, and they have lofty aspirations. But I need them to be a threat I can control in my new empire." *His new empire?* The man truly had taken his successes to heart. "This all leads me back to you," Hernán said. "When the other Spanish prudes come, they'll be looking for you. Right now, you're a perfect place-marker for the guilt of this tribe; the troop is going to assume you lost to the indís instead of losing to me. The Spaniards will kill them and save you. Meanwhile, I'll be some distance off, laying the groundwork for a new administration in this country. I won't have to worry about any more indí threats. Your fellow Spaniards will make sure of that."

I gave him a coy glance. "Sounds maybe a bit harsh," I said.

"Oh, get over it," he said, sneering. "I heard you were nasty yourself down in Cuba a few years ago."

"I could put the troops back on your trail," I said. "I'll just tell them the truth."

"Go ahead and try that. See what happens." Hernán's smile was the widest I had yet seen. I chose to ignore him. He reached for his metal helmet, grabbing it before slowly rising to his feet. "It's been a nice talk," he said, "but I'd best be going." Turning to exit the earthen cell, he stopped after only a few steps. "I hope your eye starts feeling better," he said. "It was a shame you couldn't fit it back in."

That was all I could take. "I'll come home a hero, you know. They think you're a leech, and they respect any man who fights to bring you down." I glared at him intensely. "Soon, Hernán, I'll outdo you."

"You're horribly mistaken," he said. "They pity you. Any opportunity they give you will be doomed to fail from the start." Hernán flashed his thin smile a final time and walked off to build his new empire.

Was he right? Was the expedition's misfortune all because of me?

I at last stood and escaped my thoughts. I shouted at the ships behind to follow me to shore.

Captain Núñez guided the closest raft, but he had trouble hearing my order.

He shouted forward. "What did you say, Governor?" His skipper was rowing with him at the front, and they looked dreadfully spent. Their rations must have also run thin.

"Head north!" I shouted back, pointing. "Go to the coast!"

He shook his head. "Governor... just hold on a minute, we're rowing up to you."

My ship's skipper and oarsmen heard the captain's words, so they waited accordingly for the other raft to approach our side.

Alvar Núñez smiled with a glaze over his eyes. "Can't help but think..." he made a tired grunt as he stopped rowing, "that we might be at some mass right now, since it's a Sunday." He laughed and lifted himself from the deck. It was beyond me how he kept track of the days.

"What of my words didn't you hear, Captain?" I asked.

Núñez shivered visibly in the cold air; his shirt had been used to patch the sails. "I heard it," he said. "But I noticed the ship ahead of you... just thought we should make sure they don't sail the wrong way."

I nodded. "I've already been trying to lead them in; but it won't help worrying if they're going to drift us out there too."

He frowned. "So you want to leave them?"

I shrugged. "If you want to follow me, then you'd better row your fastest."

The squat captain gave a quick nod and then motioned for his men to follow my boat.

Our rafts rowed in tandem until sunset, but Alvar Núñez was soon falling behind; his face cringed with pain every time he pulled back his oars, and his men looked no better. They were a ghastly pale, with ribs that jutted from the skin.

At last Núñez heaved in exhaustion.

"Governor," he said. "We can't keep up much longer."

"What can I do?" I asked.

His breath fluttered. "Can you throw a rope?"

"You want us to drag you?" I shot him a hard, questioning glance, and he stared at me in surprise for a moment. His dark eyes regained focus.

"That's the only way we can keep up with you."

I rubbed my face, trying to think. "Núñez, I can't make my men do twice the work to get your ship to shore; it's not fair to them."

He nodded reluctantly. "What do you think we should do then?"

"I don't know what you should do, Captain. But you're eventually going to have to reach the ports in Pánuco any way you can; I don't think we'll see you again until you do." For some reason, I felt strangely certain about this, and when the aggravated captain fell far enough behind, I couldn't distinguish his raft from the background's bluish haze.

CHAPTER 6

Stranded

———

ALVAR NÚÑEZ

La Isla de Malhado, Fall 1528

A simple urge brought me to the beach. Evening was setting in. I felt so damn cold.

What a shame it had been for our raft to rupture in the middle. What a shame for our knives, tools, and bundles to be scattered to sea. Nine men lost their lives because a poorly-built mass of wood had struck a sand barge. My co-captain, the Inspector Solis, was decaying at the bottom of the gulf.

Others began to crawl or limp onto the sand. Soon, we were all resting on our backs, our hands raw and our pants shredded. Catatonic gazes surrounded me. Hopes had been dashed by a single accident.

I needed to save my men. "Come on, let's gather some firewood," I said. "We have to keep a fire burning, or else our blood's going to go cold." No one cared to follow me; they were all exhausted. Daylight was rapidly waning.

I mustered whatever strength I had to search for dry wood. Inevitably, dryness was hard to find; the storm's rainwater had soaked the trunks and fallen branches. Some living tree limbs were suitable enough, but our axes had sunk with the raft. I was beginning to feel panicked. I realized, however, that the storm had also left dew on the leaves; even though achieving a fire felt nearly impossible, there was at least a store of drinkable water now available. I eased my aching throat with a nearby leaf and returned to the men.

Tavera, the elderly ship pilot, had already gathered the best fallen branches he could find. He organized them in a pile, and was directing a younger man as they rubbed two sticks quickly together.

Old Tavera stopped his work and addressed me. "Any luck finding dry wood?"

"Nothing we can get without an axe," I said.

Tavera cursed and threw his stick to the ground. "This is pointless then, Lope," he said to the younger man, who was aged only seventeen or so.

"There's some dew on the leaves," I said to reassure the pair. "It'll be cold tonight, but at least we won't die of thirst." I took a seat beside the worthless fire pit, turning to face Old Tavera's adolescent tag-along. "In the morning, Lope, I'll need you to scout this place out a little more. Climb a tall tree and let me know what's nearby."

"Absolutely, Captain," Lope said.

Old Tavera chuckled. "The boy doesn't know how to swim, Cap'n. Had to drag him from the shipwreck so he wouldn't drown." Tavera was an uncouth, weathered fisherman, and I liked his straight-forward speech. Lope frowned; his embarrassment was obvious.

I laughed. "Hopefully you're better on land, Lope," I said. "Otherwise, we'll have to use you as a fire-starter instead of a scout."

My humor was lost on Lope. He smiled politely, but only because I was his captain. I could see the deaths of an hour prior still bending his gaze downward. Old Tavera, on the other hand, reclined to sleep peacefully.

I too slept, but my dreams were nagged by the guilt of having let our fates fall uncertain. I tried instead to think of the Spanish sun beaming on the fields behind my childhood home.

The sun did not come out in the morning; I awoke shivering. Soon, however, a humidity pervaded the day, enough to distract me from the earlier brisk air.

"Lope, what's the lay of the land?" I asked.

He had just returned from scaling a nearby tree. "We're on an island," he said. "It's unusually flat, but you can't tell that past all this forest. The ground's got potholes that look like hoof prints; if there are cows, then the Spanish must have been here before." Lope seemed excited by the prospect. "We might even be near Pánuco..."

"Thanks, Lope," I said. But I was not so convinced by his theory: the Spanish would never settle on a flat, muggy island like this for very long. "Take a walk around the beach and see what else you can spot. Bring Tavera with you."

Hours later, the pair returned with a little dog strolling close behind.

"We found this mutt not far off," Old Tavera said. "A bit further along we realized three indís were following us. They haven't been in any hurry to catch us, though." Tavera pointed back. "They're sitting on the beach right over there. Go look if you like."

I peered down the shore. Sure enough, there were three indígenas, lightly cradling their bows. The mangy-looking islanders could have cared less whether I approached or retreated. They seemed aware of me, but unconcerned.

More distant, and clearly in motion, a separate troupe of natives advanced to meet the other three. They appeared as one hundred stalks of indí maize, filling the horizon without enough distinction to evoke recognition. But I had never been scared by crops. One hundred indígenas meant one hundred possible bows and spears, completely visible from where I stood.

"There are more on the way," I told my companions calmly.

The indígenas approached us with apathy; their lackluster nature made them all the more intimidating. Inventory-wise, we were practically helpless. Except for a few salvaged knives, we had no weapons; worse than not having weapons was the fact that we didn't have the strength to run. Despite this vulnerability, I turned around to see that some of my men were poorly attempting to flee.

"We should get out of here," Lope said, his youthful eyes wide.

"No, Lope. Stay right where you are," Tavera said. He turned to me. "What's your thought, Cap'n?"

I reflected for a moment on my previous experiences. Once, a seemingly French battalion, who would have been hostile to Spanish infantry, turned out to be a mercenary unit hired by a nearby Italian duke to help us. Another time, my army had overtaken a French barracks, but decided to let them all live; had they tried to flee or fight back, we might have reacted more violently. I wondered how these islanders would react.

"Our best move is to stand still and act friendly," I said. Lope was shaking in fear. I noticed the beads of his rosary shaking along with him; the item had somehow survived our shipwreck. An idea came to me. "Better yet, let's offer them what we have." I yelled back at my other men, most of whom had given up fleeing. "Men! Start pulling out your rosaries!"

Inquisitive glances arrived at me from all directions, but most who could chose to follow my order. Old Tavera slowly caught on. "Good thinking," he said. For lack of a rosary, he revealed a medallion from his pant leg. I myself joined the effort, unearthing the pin that had once adorned my infantry uniform.

I waved my arms at the approaching indígenas. Shouting would have provided no benefit, as their likelihood of understanding Castilian was as low as the tribes in La Florida. We hurriedly presented all the beads and bells they'd want, hoping to keep them at bay; the problem, though, was that all these remaining trinkets were personal. These weren't practical tools; these were our last pieces of home.

As soon as the indígenas saw the sun glisten off our offerings, their approach gained intrigue. Towering fixtures of an unorganized natural world were discovering the fringe artifacts of organized men. I in turn pondered the scars of their intimate terrestrial knowledge, and how their feet crossed jagged rock toward us with deserved confidence. These natives had worn themselves so firmly into the fabric of wilderness that they felt no pressure to shape it toward comfortable living. Wilderness posed no challenge to their society. And yet, like organized men, this band of locals recognized the procedures of exchange. A tall, olive man with a hairless, contoured face walked up to me. Before he could act, I held out my infantry pin. The man accepted it, but didn't linger. Instead, he reached from the satchel tied around his waist and pulled out an arrow.

I stood still, staring, waiting for him to make any further movement; he finally extended the arrow, motioning to his very own handiwork. *Here, take it*, he seemed to be expressing.

I grabbed the offering, then nodded a thank you. All the other Spaniards around me then traded their own pieces of home to receive the lifeline of a rougher land. The arrows kept coming until our hands were full. For our meager gifts to them, we had reaped abundantly. Perhaps the islanders did not understand the dual purpose of exchange after all.

The indígenas left us in peace. I found myself considering the same worries as the day before: fire, water, food, and after such a cold night, now shelter too.

"I think we might need them," I told Tavera.

"You want to rely on their help?" he asked. "Don't you realize they have all the control right now?"

"Yes, I know," I said. I ran my fingers through the same sand which had invited us. "It's a matter of survival. If we don't live through this island, then we can forget any hope of reestablishing our hold on La Florida."

"Reestablishing our hold?" Old Tavera burst into laughter. "Cap'n, that goal has long passed. We lost. The moment the Governor set our course for Nueva España, we lost whatever opportunity we had to take control." He shook his head reproachfully. "You're a soldier; I thought you had this realized."

I swallowed my spit and paused for a moment. "Why do you care if they get more control then?" I asked. "Since we're already defeated, receiving their help shouldn't matter."

"No, I still want to keep my dignity," Tavera said. "Submitting to those animals would be a loss I won't forget."

This last comment caused me to ruminate. When I was orphaned at the age of ten or twelve, I can't remember which, I quickly overcame the shame in asking for help. And, growing up in the South, with so many Muslims and Jews around me, I had even received assistance from the lowest on the Iberian Peninsula. So did these natives we had met—who had just provided us with a multitude of arrows—present any greater possibility of bringing shame? I had never been faced with the question. But when my head lacked answers, I went with my gut; my gut disagreed with Tavera's sentiment.

"Well, as your captain, I'm inclined to say we accept any help they provide. I know it's not becoming for a group of Spaniards, but it's much better than dying. In the meantime, we should do our best to get by."

The islanders indeed returned the next morning. After another cold night, their presence was especially welcome. The indígenas bombarded our camp as if ants. The islander women in particular meticulously improved our daily operations. Their first act was to configure a working fire. They had amassed dry logs for times such as these; once the flames were lit, they cooked fish for both themselves and our crew. A certain root they had pulled from shallow water was also passed around. They expressed to us through signs that the roots were very hard to pull, but that they intended to show us how, so we might collect them ourselves. Some were very big and some small, like any food, so we tried our best to ration them fairly. We followed their example in cooking the roots in leftover fish lard. I bit into mine and thought it tasted a lot like walnut. Old Tavera had until that point avoided their company out of pride; when he smelled the food, however, he sauntered over to share the natives' meal.

I genuinely enjoyed having the indígenas around. Not only for the food, though that was the major reason; the islanders kept coming back every morning and evening, bringing us more roots, fish, and even drinkable water. What I also appreciated was their overt willingness to share survival secrets: namely the root pulling. When the day arrived that they chose to teach us, I was glad to have learned a provision of consistent starch; I put the lesson into practice, yanking the roots from places I had not previously thought to search. I noticed the natives observing my technique. They were several feet back, muttering among themselves, perhaps discussing how my eyes were yet untrained or how my arms fooled them into thinking I had strength. Or perhaps they weren't commenting on me at all. Regardless, my gaze shifted to our old trinkets which were now tied around their necks, and it dawned on me how quickly they had assumed our cultural fixtures. Fitting, as we were now certainly adopting theirs.

My eyes soon shifted to a silver-rimmed green stone necklace worn by one of the males. I had not seen it before, but it was certainly Spanish. I grabbed his attention immediately.

He gave me a surprised glance and then smiled when he understood my intentions. Lifting the stone up from his chest, he examined it with admiration, and then motioned his hand away from the fire in the direction from which he had come. The islander made a grouping motion toward me with both his hands, signifying that he meant the foreigners—the Spaniards. *They're here*, his hands seemed to say. He smiled brightly.

My mouth gaped, then I rallied myself off the ground. "Lope, Tavera: come with me quickly," I said to them from across the flames. "There are other Spaniards on the island."

The indígena agreed to lead us to our countrymen. We followed him through the woods of the island, on until an opening between the branches. Wait here, he directed us; the Spaniards will come to you.

There was a flutter in my stomach. The root I had eaten barely suppressed it.

I could hear faint voices approaching, and before long I recognized them. Strained murmurs from Alonso del Castillo and the distinct speech of Captain Andrés Dorantes. My crew was not alone.

"Where's your raft?" I asked.

"It's on the beach on the island's other side," Castillo answered. "The boat has a fracture, but we managed to wrap around before it stalled. We wanted to be closer to the mainland."

The camp built by the two captains and their crew was more lived-in and shaded than my own. My pride felt stung that my fellow captains managed to guide their men safely to shore, whereas I had failed to protect several of mine from a drowning death.

I furrowed my brows. "You think it can be fixed?"

"Maybe," Castillo mused.

"I'm sure it can be," Andrés Dorantes said. "But it's taken a while, and we still have to make sure it's done right."

I sighed, at least partly relieved. Tavera, walking nearby to fill his native water jar, heard Dorantes and turned around. The old sailor interjected. "It needs to be patched?" Castillo nodded, and Old Tavera's face bulged. "God! Well, why aren't we doing it then? Let's fix this and get out of here."

"It's not that easy," Andrés Dorantes said. "We've been trying daily, but the carpenter sliced his hand and can't direct us past his accent. Nobody knows what they're doing."

Tavera smiled. "You're lucky I do."

Andrés frowned and Castillo looked over at me to confirm.

"He does," I said. "He's been a port-rat his whole life."

"Come to supervise me if you want," Tavera said. "I'll patch it."

Andrés gave a reassured humph. He shouted at his little brother. "Diego, do you and Estevanico want to help him mend the hole?" Diego nodded in assent.

Old Tavera, with the help of Diego and the Dorantes family's morisco slave, patched the raft within a few hours. The night then went by without a hitch before we awoke and put the boat to sea. A couple of our men joined Tavera for the test on how well his repair could sail.

They took it out a fair distance, with one or two rowers on each side. The water was manageable, but not easy. One of the waves, effortlessly it seemed, wrapped itself around both sides of the raft. The bow was lifted dramatically, but it didn't capsize. Instead, when the front lifted, Tavera was sent back to the other end of the ship without a proper grip, and his head struck the edge of the boat. I could see the other skipper shouting uproariously, saying he needed to get him back to shore; but soon, however, the next wave came and tore the immobile Tavera off the deck. To save him from drowning, a fellow man jumped off to swim him to shore, while those that stayed onboard were met with a terribly large wave that split through the hull. Water poured through the crack, the very same that had been repaired; so, before the next wave would surely drown them, the remaining men on the ship escaped to shore, leaving the boat to fracture from the middle. They dragged Tavera onto the sand, trying to revive him; but the terrible gash across his head was obvious. Tavera had not initially drowned; he had first been knocked cold.

Seeing the old man dead, I was reminded of the passing of my brothers. I was left toughened and scarred, and I felt I knew how to scar. It dawned on me that building colonies had no different a lure than war, and I had arrived simply to fulfill my prior calling.

I dwelt over my thoughts on the sand beside Castillo and Andrés Dorantes.

"We're going to have to spend the winter here," Castillo said. "There's no way to swim with the water getting colder."

Andrés stared at him, truly soured by the loss of their boat. "It might be cold, Castillo, but the mainland's not that far. Another month and it could be impenetrable. But that's another month."

"It may not be far for us," Castillo said, "but some of the other men... well, they can't even stand up, let alone handle the water."

Andrés Dorantes shrugged. A fire should have been burning, but we felt no pull to preserve ourselves.

I brooded until my words coalesced. "Why not send the men who can?" I asked.

Castillo and Andrés looked at me, and for a moment they thought it over. Castillo shook his head. "I don't feel good about that. We shouldn't split up the men when the odds of finding each other again are so low."

Castillo had over-analyzed my plan. "You misunderstand me," I said. "We only need to send a few, just the most able-bodied who can manage themselves. They can find Nueva España and then return here, bringing us back in the spring."

Andrés Dorantes gave me a confident nod. "I like that idea," he said. "Using scouts would make sure our time here's not wasted."

Castillo again frowned. "I'm not for it. I think we should all stay together."

"Well, that's two captains for and one against," I said. "Castillo, we can pick as few men as possible, but we should still send some."

Castillo nodded reluctantly. "Alright," he said. "You all can pick the men; I have no interest in it." The slender captain rose from the sand and walked back to camp.

Andrés Dorantes and I discussed for several more minutes. We thought of Figueroa, and Méndez, and Don Astudilloi, and the Portuguese carpenter Fernández, all of whom had experience and reliability. Fernández especially had been hopeless since injuring his carpentry hands; scouting had the potential to give him more purpose, we felt. Our current dilemma was undoubtedly also affecting my own sense of purpose. A winter trapped on an island, managing a group of hopeless souls did not provide the same fulfillment as claiming La Florida surely could.

"What about your brother?" I asked. "He's strong, smart enough."

"No, I don't want to send him." Andrés seemed insistent. "He's staying here."

"Fair enough," I said. "That's all we should need."

By morning, we ushered our four scouts into the channel to the mainland. Two islander guides were in the lead. I noticed them all cringe as they stepped into the frigid water, and I wondered if they could make it through the coming winter.

CHAPTER 7

The Starving Crew

SOTOMAYOR THE CAMP MASTER

Texas, Late Fall 1528

Perhaps the Governor felt guilty for having left the other rafts to their own fates. Perhaps he believed his burden was to atone for this wrong. More likely, he was morose from the air of failure that pervaded him.

The Governor peered with his working eye behind our boat. I followed his gaze to see another boat, one of ours, being pulled by the heavy winds and rains into a maze of small rivers. "Could we possibly reach that raft?" the Governor asked our pilot.

Our pilot frowned. "We'd really be going out of our way."

"Hmm." The Governor's face strained. Captain Pantoja nodded in agreement with the pilot; the Governor, noticing this, settled on his own decision. "I can't let it struggle in my plain sight," he said to the pilot. "But we'd have to go after it alone, skipper. We could drop the others off first and then retrieve it... Can you do that with me?"

Without hesitation, the pilot agreed. "I'll let our men off at this cove, Governor."

Captain Pantoja sat beside his immediate superior, his concern apparent. "Whose boat is it?" he asked.

"It's under the head monk and the Comptroller," the Governor said, lifting himself from off the deck. "Comptroller Enriquez is a young leader, a man learning under my shadow. But he's struggling on that ship, Pantoja, and so I feel compelled as his mentor to go after it." He turned to the captain. "In case anything goes wrong, I'll need a strong mind, someone who will be safe on the beach. Can you take my post while I retrieve these men?"

Captain Pantoja nodded, and his forehead lost its strain. His concern had dissipated.

The Governor smiled. "Good," he said. He then called over his page to make the reassignment official. The page produced a book, barely intact through all our trekking, and wrote the details of the new replacement. He started coughing, sickened from cold winds, while the Governor told him to write Pantoja's name on the sheet.

"Thank you, Governor," Pantoja said, a grim look on his face. "I'll take good care of these men until you get back."

"You're the most qualified man I know, Captain," the Governor said. "I trust you more than anyone to get these men to Nueva España."

"I will, Governor." The two men embraced each other for a brief moment.

Both officers were older than most in the crew, and the Governor considered age the measure of experience; but even though I too was among the aging, I did not agree. Regardless, when he addressed the crew, I expressed no qualms about his plan, and neither did anyone else.

Our boat hovered near shore, where we all disembarked as the Governor had ordered; we then unloaded every empty sack and pious man's rosary onto the beach where we prepared to stay. Only our *Adelantado* would be leaving to rescue the drifting ship, joined by the pilot and his coughing page, a boy no older than twenty. I had no clue why the boy joined them. How such lemmings survive childhood amazed me.

The trio sailed eastward, into the maze of waterways in which the head monk and comptroller's ship had gotten lost. I watched from the beach, keeping my eyes on the boat until it became obscured.

A powerful northern wind pulled me from my sleep. It was raining hard, and I went to find cover under one of the coves that graced the shoreline. There I stood uncomfortably through the night.

The rains softened by midday, so our temporary commander, Captain Pantoja, brought us out to a point where the eastern rivers were visible. Our view was unobstructed, but neither the Governor's boat nor the Fray's were anywhere to be seen. Had they drifted, or had they sunk?

Some of the men fell to their knees in defeat; our only remaining monk wept for his stranded companions as he clenched his temple, muttering a curse to God. "How could You let this happen! They were Your servants!"

We waited another two days before considering these two boats and their men lost for good.

Mutual decision led us to remain in the ideal grove of trees placed right against the coast. Smoke rose into the sky from a native campfire; on the day we approached the source, the people of the coast were dismantling their huts. They were frantically carrying collapsed materials onto their canoes, taking off without ever quashing their fires. Had they noticed us and gotten scared? Or was there another reason for abandonment? Despite the nagging uncertainty, I was pleased to have been left a habitable home.

"Let's take this place while there's still a fire burning," I said. "We've been handed a gift."

And a gift it was. The coastal forest invited several animals to the nearby waters: crawfish, bass, and fish with long whiskers. These woods had sturdy trees, some of them protected enough from the shoreline rains to have remained dry; this meant good shelter, and consistent fire. With fire, you can boil water and cook meat. Fire meant life. Especially in winter.

Captain Pantoja agreed with my settlement plan, and we beached the raft. Ever since leaving for La Florida, my role was as the expedition's camp master. Every encampment built by the expedition went under my direction, and I resolved the men's disputes when they occurred in our living spaces. My work was a lot like running a plantation.

I directed us to build the camp using chopped timber (because the natives left no huts), and I instructed the men in the best way to set the lodges. "Build them in a clearing," I said, "because we sure don't need the trees to fall on them." It felt nice to have some control over my fate; however, I hadn't thought about much except food, water, and safety for the past year. Control was secondary to it all.

Captain Pantoja, on the other hand, quickly revealed that he craved power even when physical needs should have prevailed. He maintained a strict grip on the camp, rationing food in a way that hearkened to an army battalion. Our lives were made increasingly routine. Pantoja set up a unit for every sort of task: a group for boiling water, a group for fishing, a group for going to find nuts and fruits in the woods. And all this was managed with a cruel bite, a deeply discouraging presence to run our daily labors. His exchanges were full of intimidation, his demeanor overtly professional; despite this, his beard looked just as uneven and mangy as ours. I grew tired of having him stand over my shoulders. With the task of building shelters completed, though, I had no further sway.

As winter approached, the daily humidity comforted us less frequently. Pantoja assigned me to picking berries and nuts, but they were quickly proving harder to come by. Other men complained that the fish, too, were fleeing their usual spots. Winter was shriveling our food supply.

"Keep looking, Corral," Pantoja barked. "The men are relying on you for their rations."

"Of course, sir," said Don Corral. He was a mild man in his fifties whose son had died the summer before. "It's just that my hands are losing their feeling with all this fruitless digging. None of the nuts or berries provide much sustenance."

"So what are you suggesting we do then?" Captain Pantoja gave him a belittling stare. "Should we abandon our reliable fire source and wander around for greener pastures?"

Dejected, Don Corral shook his head. I spoke up. "Captain, I know I was in favor of this location from the beginning," I said. "However, Don Corral makes a strong point: if we let ourselves become complacent here, we'll have less of a chance to find a new settlement once winter truly takes its hold."

Captain Pantoja scowled. "Next time, I'll hear your opinion when it's asked for, camp master. And as for leaving, you both can forget about that plan. Get back to scavenging."

I walked back into the woods angrily, and Don Corral sauntered. Bark jabbed at my hands as I peeled it from the trees, and worms writhed between my fingers as I snatched them from the ground. Neither tasted pleasant. The men were displeased with their rations.

Don Corral's hands grew purple and dry, and his deep cough worsened.

"We need to assert ourselves," I said to him. "Pantoja's desire to be right is going to kill us."

Don Corral said nothing in return. He shrugged off my words; his mild manner was afraid to consider a dismissal of the captain's orders.

Don Corral died in his sleep that very night. I was determined to confront Pantoja the following day.

"Captain…" He was standing near the campfire, facing the wall of trees which surrounded the lodges. He turned to look at me, and I could feel his annoyance. "The men are done with you," I said. "You run this place like we're prisoners, like a labor camp, but there's no reason to. You have no direction in what you're doing."

Pantoja smiled, still picking away at the beetle leg stuck in his teeth. "Where'd you muster that?"

"I'm not finished, so don't interrupt," I said. My broad body stood firm. He stopped picking his teeth. "We're barely scraping by as is, but your treatment has made it that much harder. You're utterly blind to the hell happening around you… You need to step down, Captain; we refuse to listen to you any longer."

Pantoja stared at me coldly; his smile had dropped. "If you didn't have my orders, camp master, you'd be trying to cook poison oak. You all need me. You're helpless sons of bitches, and the world never gives much help. It's a wonder how I even keep you all alive." He paused. "Well, some of you, that is."

I outweighed the man by a lot, and my hit sent him to the ground. He wiped the blood off his chin.

"Get up," I said. "Or are you also a helpless son of a bitch?"

I allowed him to lift himself off the ground, then watched him slowly bring his fists up to each side. He tried to catch me by surprise, swinging left, so I dodged and punched him again. He was fairly sly for his age.

Men began gathering to watch us brawl, yet no one dared intervene. We exchanged blows for the short while that his hits landed. Nevertheless, the poor bastard couldn't hit farther than his foot; his strength did not last long against my heavy hand. Each powerful impact beat the blood from his face as if it never belonged there. His eyes started to swell up, and though he managed to stand, I punched him until he no longer could, his head crashing against the fire-pit. No scream escaped his lips.

I dragged him up, not meaning for his head to burn in the flames; but when I saw the way it was charred, the way his body sagged, I knew he had not survived.

The company waited by Captain Pantoja for a few moments, not sure what to do with him.

"Okay," I finally said. "He's dead."

I pulled him by the legs a few feet outside the camp, then went to grab a shovel; there was a hand-made one in my lodge, and I took it over to the spot, beginning to dig. A half hour later, I had made a grave for the Captain, so I dropped him inside and patted the dirt over his corpse. Our last remaining monk gave a meager eulogy, and then we forgot about the whole ordeal.

When everyone awoke after sleeping past sunrise, the grave had been overturned and the Captain's body was nowhere to be found.

"Christ!" I said after looking all over. "Do you suppose he just crawled out and walked?"

"I don't have a clue," said López.

The company, abandoning all other pursuits, searched the woods to discover what had happened to Captain Pantoja. It was late when someone found traces of blood stretching deeper into the wood. He called us over, and our entire crew moved with him along the crimson line until we reached a clearing in the trees. The Captain's body lay across the ground, facing the sky; he definitely had not walked there himself. Everything about him was the same as the day before, battered head and all, but a large cut had been ripped out of his left thigh. His pants were still on, though not where the slice had been made.

God Almighty... the wind seemed to whisper. Someone had dug him out just to eat from his leg.

An old man named Gonzalo brought everybody together to discuss the atrocity.

"Whoever ate the Captain's thigh," he said, pausing to settle his shock, "is going to be found out by us at some point. So I suggest, if that man is you, that you run away from camp tonight." He stared at every man with equal mistrust. "Start swimming or sprinting in any direction you want to; but as soon as we realize who you are, and that you've left the camp, we're going to kill you."

That night, I inevitably stayed awake to see if someone would risk an escape; surely enough, no one did.

At a meeting the next afternoon, I was on the lookout for somebody to crack under the emotional weight of his guilt. It didn't happen. Neither did it happen the next day, or the following, or any of the days for another week. Each paranoid man had abandoned his lodgings, and the camp, moving gracefully to his own solitary corner of the forest to tend to his needs. Tension in the woods rose to an unbelievable height; all the while our hunger was rising. Even the worms and beetles seemed to be sparse. The winds, too, were now wintry brisk. A man's system, when starved of nutrition, can only fight harsh conditions for so long before it fails. The company was separating itself, perhaps from temptation. Each individual was blocking his view of the other men.

I spent endless days tending to my own fire, using it to boil stream water and soften bark. Every berry was now truly frozen over, inedible; the small game had dispersed. My mind was losing its grip.

Why was I staying here? Not matter how much I wanted to, I simply could not flee. If I tried to leave the forest, on a hand-made canoe or by any other means, then another man would be waiting for me, lurking behind to catch me like prey. I witnessed it firsthand. Gonzalo left before he might become a cannibal himself, and a vulture named Palacios pursued him; they fought, and Gonzalo somehow struck him dead. He cried because he didn't know what to do with the dead man's corpse.

López, not a week later, killed Gonzalo and fed on both bodies.

Ruiz soon ate López.

Esquivel ate Ruiz. He also ate Bartolomé.

Bartolomé had eaten another man the day prior.

Someone dug through the graves to find food, but he was similarly killed.

I can't remember if I participated.

Our camp was a stone's throw below the depths of hell, and eventually there were just two men left in the forest.

CHAPTER 8

Isla de Malhado

ALONSO DEL CASTILLO

Island of the Han and Cavoques, 1529

Life on the island turned sour for us the moment their children became sick. Every winter prior, the natives on both sides managed to collect enough roots and fish to sustain themselves and their younger tribe members; they never suffered significant losses even in the weakest seasons. But this year, to our luck, the humble isle was plagued by the worst storms that the inhabitants expressed to ever have endured. Since powerful storms tend to land-lock flocks of people in densely-vegetated groves, the ability to catch fish and pull shore-side roots is limited enough to deplete a child. For these natives, it took over half their children.

"Christ," muttered Núñez, "it's one thing for grown men and women to die. But all these children... there's nothing worse." His voice had grown distractingly hoarse, soaked by the continuous rain. "The parents are starting to blame us, you know."

"Well, they must realize we're just as hungry and sick as they are," I said. "And dead too. Those of us not already dead will be if this keeps up any longer." I looked my colleague in the eye. "You should probably stop making those mad-dashes to the beach, Núñez. The roots aren't worth the exposure."

He chuckled. The torrent that came through the trees was hitting his face, while the larger drops that were collecting on the leaves soon fell to collect on his forehead. He seemed unperturbed. "Good point. I won't grab any more roots. I'll have to make due with stealing your food, I suppose." Núñez barely contained his smile, waiting for my reaction. I was about to return banter of my own, but he entered a coughing fit and forgot about the whole joke. "You're right," Núñez said after his last cough resounded. "I should wait awhile to leave the woods again."

I nodded, pleased.

By the time the winter rains finally subsided, sixty-five of our Spaniards had joined the weak-stomached and sickened six feet below. We were no longer a crew; just fifteen foreigners scrambling out of a rut. The indís were comparably derailed. Both tribes of the island could not hide their change in temperament. They were non-functional, beside themselves with sobs for their children; yet amidst the misery, their newfound disdain for us was evident. We had caused these deaths. Our arrival spurred the storms.

I'm not sure if they actually believed this; regardless, at the very least, they chose to recollect in full detail the drain on resources we had for so long been. We had turned from welcome, suckling dependents into pure competition for the limited food that could have saved their actual kin. So yes, they were angry. I braced myself to see what they would do about it.

The Cavoques and Han—as the two island tribes were called—gathered together to discuss their foreign policy. Their leaders spent the daylight hours around an unlit fire in what appeared to be a heated discussion (the words were not exchanged, however, until both sides had wept ceremoniously to grieve the losses of the other).

A Cavoques spoke. "We appreciate your gifts to us. After the passing of our chief, it meant much to receive your good gesture."

The Han Chief smiled with a nod. While I now understood most of the Cavoques tongue, I hadn't spent enough time with the Han tribe to comprehend what their chief replied.

Another Cavoques leader, helping to fill in for his departed chief, responded. "You bring up an important issue. But I do believe they should face punishment."

My ears perked wider. *Punishment? Us?*

The Han Chief, however, adamantly shook his head. His tone grew serious when he spoke.

So the Cavoques responded. "Perhaps that is true. The strangers would not also have died if the storm was their doing; I am not so foolish to think that. But their greed over winter has left us all childless. They at least need to make amends."

To this, the Han Chief agreed.

The two tribes thus decided to implement us as able servicemen in the process of restoring their camps to a sufficient build and food security. We were to patch lodges, harvest roots, and catch fish as our recompense, all for an amended lower ration. Gone were the days of their unmatched provisions.

The tribal leaders discussed how to portion our services. Most of the surviving men had been from my raft, and, according to our native hosts, we were to remain with the Cavoques who had found us. But additionally, seeing as the Cavoques had recently lost their chief (whose old, frail body had succumbed to the storm), it was agreed that they would also receive the help of all but one from Captain Núñez's raft. The Spaniard who was to remain with the Han tribe was Captain Núñez himself.

I doubt the tribes had any intention to make our lives so difficult by splitting one of our men from the rest; they likely had only wanted for the Han to have some benefit in the arrangement, and they figured Núñez a decent compromise. But this made any plans to move forward with our journey extremely challenging. I was about to protest this separation, but Núñez waved me down. "I can manage," he said. "It's best to keep them in good spirits." Núñez departed to the Han's side of the island that afternoon.

Núñez raised a decent point, but I nonetheless worried for our futures. Whenever the fourteen of us decided upon a time to attempt leaving, we would need to find a way to reach him beforehand. Leaving him behind was not an option. Considering this inconvenience, Captain Dorantes and I decided to continue laboring until our brains mustered the best way to the mainland. Should we tell the natives and seek their help? Should we attempt yet another raft-building enterprise on our own?

I spent my nights with the members of a Cavoques household, always exhausted after the days pulling through the sand and spear-jabbing the water. The family was large, with extended members all under the same roof.

The eldest grandson in this house's core family was nearing adulthood, but had gradually slowed in his responsibilities that otherwise should have been increasing. His injured leg was the cause. Tree bark shrapnel had propelled into his shin during the winter rainstorms, and with little opportunity for assistance, he left the rather minor wound alone. Had I known this family earlier, I would have drawn from my parents' medical experience to advise the grandson to treat his cut. But as the rot progressed unattended, the spread of purplish tint had lifted his family from mild concern into genuine desperation. Wasting no further time, they wisely called upon the medicine man.

The Cavoques medicine man was the most vital piece of their tribal life. While the chief (or temporary leaders, now) might often be led to discuss inter-tribal issues or to attend to wider matters, the medicine man was a continual mold around the camp's daily function. He always held his fingers on its pulse.

When the medicine man walked into the dwelling, he struck me as the sole rose-colored and weighty person on the island. He had clearly been minding his own health.

My host family beckoned the grandson to sit before their guest and display his wound. The medicine man examined the leg, then swiftly revealed a thin knife, crafted from stone, and applied it to the area of infection, cutting small holes all around the swollen part of the leg. In a method that shocked me, he placed his mouth down toward the cuts, muttering quietly to subside the young man's hysteria. With several heavy slurps, the medicine man sucked the infection from the leg and stood to spit it on the ground. He then took a dry stick, lit it in the lodge's fire, and used the flame to seal shut the incisions on the leg. The boy yelled out in pain, but the medicine man once again calmed him.

"All better," he said, turning to the family. "Another moon and he won't feel anything when he runs."

"Thank you," said the grandfather, a meek, slender fellow of comparable age to the healer.

"I would appreciate your compensation," the medicine man espoused tonelessly.

"Of course." The grandfather rallied the members of the family, and over the next several minutes, they proceeded to present the medicine man with nearly every item in their lodge. Each tool, bow, blanket, decorative flair, and personal knickknack was laid at the feet of the man who had simply performed his duty.

"Don't look so shocked," the grandmother told me. "This is what's expected when the shaman successfully saves your kin. My grandson's life is worth far more than this, anyway."

"Of course," I responded in Cavoques, my delivery modeled after the grandfather's. "I'll get to work now; I've stuck around too long watching."

"Yes, that'd be best," the grandmother affirmed with a smile. "Just bring your catch directly to us tonight. The other families never gripe with those who've just paid for health."

As I walked over to my duties, I wondered whether I could do the same for my family. None of my parents' patients had ever parted with their entire life's bounty before. It was difficult to imagine a Spaniard making that trade so easily.

Our small company returned as the sun set, our catch and harvest slung over our backs. Before we could disburse to each home, though, four women ran out of the largest hut in the village.

"Those are the medicine man's four wives," Andrés Dorantes whispered. "I wonder what happened." The wives darted around to the different Cavoques families. Two were weeping furiously.

"He's fallen dead!" They shouted. "He's dead!"

The Cavoques peeled out of their homes and tried to reassure the women, though they also keenly strode to his lodge to investigate.

"Should we follow?" I asked Andrés.

"No, let's wait," he said. The entire tribe had seemingly entered the departed healer's home; yet the wives, who felt no need to torture themselves with the same sight, wept outside the entrance. The Cavoques eventually emerged, disgruntled, with some bickering among themselves and others woefully depressed.

An angry woman approached us. "We're trying to figure out how you did this! You're lucky we didn't find

any marks on him, or else we would have every right..."
She marched off.

Diego Dorantes slowly broke into a laugh. He turned
to me and Andrés. "You mean to tell me one wife didn't
stab him for sleeping with the others?"

Andrés Dorantes practically pushed his brother back.
"Keep quiet, Diego. They might kill us over this."

Andrés was wise to watch his words, but I must say I too
wondered what killed the medicine man. Was it disease?
Overexertion in bed? Certainly it wasn't starvation.

Moments after the angry woman left, a Cavoques
leader approached our small squadron of Spaniards.

"There's no need to worry," he said. "The leaders know
you had nothing to do with this. But I recommend not
attending his ceremony tonight; some of our own aren't
as convinced. They said they want retribution, though I
got them to agree to a fair trade-off: your best men will
become our medicine men until we can invite a new one
from a different tribe."

The Cavoques leader hid his smile at our dumb-
founded faces.

He continued. "You may not have much to do at first,
but it is an as-needed role, so pick your men soon. And
don't expect the same rewards usually given. This is for
you to return our kindness, not to receive more of it."

Andrés and Diego were quite stunned, so I spoke up.
"Understood. Thank you."

Though we'd been assured more time to prepare, the natives had an opportunity to test our medical prowess.

My household grandmother awoke me before the light of dawn and announced that her grandson's procedure had only done so much. "You need to help him," she said. "The medicine man failed us. My boy's dying, and now it's your people's job to heal him."

I rubbed the grogginess out of my eyes and uttered a short response. She left me and I sauntered after her, reaching the corner of the lodge where the boy lay still. The sight of him ended my sloth.

"You weren't exaggerating," I told her. "He does seem to be dying."

I had learned enough from observing my parents to know when an infection was expanding. Even without my childhood experiences, I still would have been able to see the boy's feverish skin, and to hear his unintelligible murmurs. He was delirious and halfway elsewhere.

I wanted to say, "I'm not sure if I can save him, but I'll at least do better than the medicine man": yet this claim, even, would have misled my hosts. His illness was a conundrum. I felt very little confidence in my ability to save the boy's life. So little, in fact, that even though the late healer's treatment had not aligned with what I knew to be medicine, I felt less inclined to call upon my own brains than to request his return from the dead. A month earlier, perhaps, I could have mustered the skills to end his affliction; yet at this point, unfortunately, it had progressed too far, and my only viable solution was to attempt surgical amputation. I wanted greatly to avoid that outcome. So instead of reassuring words, I told the grandmother, "I need to gather the other men. We'll be back within an hour, and between us, maybe we'll find a solution."

"Hurry," she said, white with worry.

I ran to the village edge where we daily went to labor. Morning was on its way, so I expected the other Spaniards to arrive momentarily. *The first few men you see,* my brain told me, *you bring back with you. Forget about picking the "best"; the doctors are no more.*

"Diego," I said to the younger Dorantes. "Come with." Diego joined me, as did the next two men. *One more,* I thought.

The next man was Asturiano, a missionary who had been removed from the Franciscans for controversial, supposedly heretical views. What exactly they were I did not know and did not care to. Trivial bickering among zealots was all. Asturiano was our last holy man, and so I hesitated to involve him. Medicine doesn't mix well with the mission.

Seeing no other men, I had to acquiesce. "Asturiano. Follow me."

We five false doctors thus turned our backs to the vast gulf sunrise and walked toward the Cavoques.

The boy was nearly dead. Several women had gathered around him and already displayed impatience with our perceived tardiness. They were speaking so fast I could not understand them; the meaning, though, was obvious: "Can you freeloaders help this child already?"

Diego spoke to answer but quickly quieted his words. "Castillo," the young man whispered to me, "we could try everything we know on the kid, but he's still going to die. What do you think his family will do to us?"

"I don't know," I said, "but it won't be good." The women, indeed, looked coolly displeased.

Asturiano, who had been leaning against the wall of the lodge, stepped out toward us. He ignored the Cavoques' gazes. "You mind if I try with the boy?"

I raised a brow. "What exactly?"

"I want to lay a hand on the injury. He needs to be prayed for." Asturiano, a rather hairless and tall half-Basque, stood with no remorse for his suggestion. Was he accustomed to people accepting blinded faith?

"No, I won't let you make a mockery out of us," I said, wiping some sweat from the bridge of my nose. It was getting hot with so many people in the room. "If you pray over the boy, Asturiano, these people are going to expect something. And it'll fail."

Asturiano's stance hardly dropped. "Alright," he nodded. "Let me know when your other plans fail, too. You might want some prayer then."

The women in the room, antsier than ever, must have assumed our talk was an argument. This they did not appreciate. "Stop the distractions," the most energetic woman said. "We had an agreement, but here you are bickering!" She rose and went toward the room's opening. "I'm going to have a word with our elders. Don't expect to be eating until this boy gets well. You've taken enough already." She exited, and an awful feeling settled over us.

Diego Dorantes looked frantic. "Castillo, I overheard the women speaking a while ago. We could press a hot stone against his leg like the medicine man did."

I shook my head. "No, heat's good for closing wounds but not for removing infection." I thought over all the medical memories of my youth. There was nothing I knew to do. But no food? If we couldn't save this boy, then could we really not eat? I looked over at his grandmother; she had been crying, but now stoically held his hand with the grace of an experienced soul. There was no way I could amputate her boy's leg in front of her. His death would remain just as likely, but he would be left separated where once intact. I swallowed my pride and addressed Asturiano. "We have to try everything. Asturiano, go ahead and pray for the boy."

The missionary approached the dying child, and I exited the room. Slumping against the outside of the lodge, I held my head in waiting: desperation in fighting the inevitable was a shame I'd rather not witness.

An hour later, the women began filing out of the lodge. The grandmother, nearly the last to walk out, was now crying again. I observed more closely. There seemed to be a tone of relief I had not expected. Asturiano walked out after her.

"Asturiano? Did you?" I scanned his eyes, and he smiled.

"See for yourself, Castillo." The half-Basque tilted his head to the entryway.

I began walking in, but I stopped myself. "Wait, Asturiano. How did you do this? How did this work?"

He turned back to me. "I didn't do anything, really. I let Him act through me."

Bewildered, I entered to see that the boy had survived. The evidence before me upturned my concept of medicine. For the first time, a Holy Man had not taken credit for his master's work; for the first time, I saw what felt like that master's work.

CHAPTER 9

Don Alvar the Merchant

ALVAR NÚÑEZ

The Texas Mainland, 1530

I was too ill to rise and join their escape. My company walked right past me, so close I could almost hear them speak; their relationship with the Cavoques had further soured, and they chose to leave without due warning. Had they searched and failed to find me? A simple walk, and I would still be with my men. Nonetheless, I reassured myself, assuming their swim to the mainland was a necessary step I did not have the strength to take. My condition indeed appeared so awful that the Han considered me a burden. I did not labor. Thoughts kept blurring with every fever dream, becoming so frequent they felt as natural as sleep.

I eventually regained the strength to be put back to work, laboring for the Han and even the Cavoques when they desired it. A season arrived of tugging at the cane reeds in search of roots, and a season of stepping on hard oyster shells. The Han spent their oyster-picking season on the mainland shore, and they of course brought me along. Daily missteps irrevocably sliced the soles of my feet against the jagged beaches; the natives were probably punishing me for my months as their burden, yet they did not understand how much more this labor drained my ability. If I continued with this intense physicality, my body would surely fall back into sickness. I tried to reason with the Han, but they insisted I keep working to the fullest. Escape to the mainland woods was my only saving grace.

So on a warm evening in late summer, while most of the Han prepared to return to the island, I stole away toward the woods with nothing beside a scrap of animal hide.

The Charrucans, as they called themselves, lived a manageable distance inland from the oyster beds; they often visited with the Han during their oyster season, and in every instance they treated me with more kindness than any village before. Additionally, they knew how to speak in the Han language, freeing me from the pressure to learn another. They were my best possible destination. In the middle of the night, I reached the outskirts of their woods, where I rested until morning. I waited for the Charrucans to awake before entering their village. They accepted me almost immediately, but it seemed like the tribe did not have any real need for an additional worker. For more than a week, I went without laboring in hardly any way, which did not ease the mind of a man in my precarious situation.

The Charrucans were in many ways similar to the other indígenas I had met; they had one wife per man, a general lack of care for the old, and an earnest love of their children. They also worshiped in true pagan fashion, and both husbands and wives slept freely with whomever they pleased. I had even seen two men steal off into the night together. The act disgusted me, but how could I cast judgment when they were to be my saviors?

With autumn drawing near, these woodland natives finally approached me to begin a task they had recently designed. It had been created especially for me from the kindness of their hearts. I was speechless: not only were they welcoming me, but they were deliberately accommodating my situation.

The Charrucans had tribal leaders, structured similarly to the Cavoques who had hosted my companions. The oldest explained my new position. "We have an abundant store of shells that are vital to every nation along the coast," he said in the Han tongue. "But despite this, we lack many important items: we have very few hides, flint, and tassels, among other valuables." To my ears, what they lacked sounded far more desirable than what they currently possessed. Perhaps shells held more value than I imagined. "We typically wait for others to visit us before trading our shells for their items. None of us wants to leave his family for very long, so we rarely go to them." The elder paused, thinking of the translation from his native Charrucan. "You don't have the same scruples holding you in place. You provide us a rare opportunity: there are several tribes who want these shells but who almost never come to the coast. You will be our traveling merchant."

Had I heard him correctly? "Traveling?" I asked.

"Yes," he said. "You'll go alone with a large supply of shells. Some nations aren't too far away, but those are the people we see more often. The ones who will offer the best trades are a many days' walk away. You'll return with what we know to be fair."

"Of course," I said, wondering what might be considered fair. "Thank you."

"Thank you too," he said. "You'll be doing us a favor."

Whether the Charrucans realized it or not, this arrangement favored me far more heavily. After only a few trips, I would learn the lay of the land, and then I could freely pursue the other Spaniards. Beyond that, I was safe: no westward tribe would ruin their relationship with the Charrucans by putting my life at risk. I had been given a guaranteed path home.

"What should we call you?" the elder asked me.

"Don Alvar," I said. For the first time in my life, I was taking personal advantage of a linguistic divide. I could finally be a "Don." In years prior, I had used language to the benefit of my Spanish troop. Our enemies spoke French, our allies spoke Fiorentino, and the locals spoke a language which combined the two. As a soldier, I always strove to learn these forms of communication potentially vital to my survival; I soon learned the tongues of the enemies, allies, and locals. I then took this task a step further. Often delegated to translation, I found ways to manipulate messages for the benefit of the Spaniards. A lot can be lost or gained in communication, and my new merchant task would also be fully served by this skill. I would need to quickly acquire the local tongues, almost as if my life depended on it. If my business relations failed from miscommunication, then perhaps my life would indeed be in danger.

I loaded a simple sack with as many seashells and cockles as the elders wanted me to carry, then I set out to the southwest in hopes of returning with their desired goods. Fallen leaves crunched under my bare feet, while the brisk wind kept a sweat from breaking across my forehead. Only an animal cloth, the one taken from the Han islanders, covered my lower half—the rest was left naked to the elements.

I traveled alone for several days without seeing another soul among the woods. I began to doubt how well I was following the Charrucans' directions. There was an undeniable risk in walking through the country without a guide or interpreter, as random encounters could escalate, and I had no way of determining a friend from a potential enemy. But for the sake of eventually reaching the others in the company, I ignored fearful thoughts; I instead cleared my mind to prepare for what might lie ahead.

My first trade was a resounding success. The Mendicans, a mainland tribe enshrouded by deep forest, presented me with some thin animal hides, tassels made from deer hair, and red dye pulverized from ocher. I bartered off all the shells I had been given in exchange for a significant amount of these goods; this single exchange would be enough to provide my Charrucan hosts with everything the season required. They were delighted by my success. As soon as I returned, they promised to make me their merchant for as long as I wanted. I found myself blushing, very proud of my work. The Charrucans spent the day celebrating me and what I accomplished in such a short time; I caught myself joining in this excitement, for I rarely was given recognition at this high level. When the Spanish army had years ago honored me for my bravery, it had been a solemn, professional event. No one had ever reveled in my achievements before.

I considered departing soon, going off to find the survivors of my company. However, the highs of celebration were strong in my thoughts. I also knew little about my surroundings. Not all tribes would be this inviting, and I did not know how to navigate between them. Besides, a better developed reputation would undoubtedly help on my lonely journey westward. If I was to thrive on my own, I needed to first take the time to become a master merchant.

The Charrucans decided I should not travel during the winter, simply because the personal risks were far too great. I thus stayed in the Charrucan woods for two months on end, trying to improve in every way possible. From engaging with the people each day, I became highly proficient in their tongue; beyond that, they taught me necessary trade phrases in every nearby language. It was common practice for the wives of native men in the region to be from another tribe, so formerly Mendican and Deaguanes women spoke openly with me in their childhood tongues. I learned to engage back in a combination of Charrucan, Mendican, and Deaguanes phrases. Soon, I separated these sounds in my head; I knew what to say and when.

Winter turned into a fruitful spring. It was perhaps April, though definitely the year 1531; I had tried to keep track. Given my early success with the Mendicans, I decided to return to them for the season's first trade.

I reasonably expected the same hides, tassels, and dyes that they had offered before. This time, however, the Mendicans were noticeably light on hides. Other than the heavy furs they personally wore, what few disposable hides the Mendicans did possess were of lesser quality than before.

"Where have all your hides gone?" I asked in my broken Mendican.

"They haven't gone anywhere," said a man whose face was painted in red ocher. "They just haven't arrived yet. We get them from the nation who sends the North Merchant: he usually arrives a week or two from now each year."

"Oh," I said. "Well, a lighter trade will have to do for now. I'll come back later when the hides have arrived."

Giving away much less in shells, I returned to the Charrucans with some dyes. About a month later, I circled around again to the Mendicans. To my surprise, the North Merchant they had spoken of was still living in their midst, remaining long past when most other visitors leave their foreign hosts. The Mendicans informed me he wanted to speak with me; he had been waiting for my arrival.

The North Merchant was tall and brawny, denser in muscle than any of the Mendicans. His head was bald on one side, while hair grew freely on the other. It was obvious that he came from a different people; he had lighter complexion, fuller features, and a hide of better warmth than any I had seen. He did not wear the hide, owing to the rising temperature, but let it sit beside him for later use on his journeys. His skin appeared very dry.

I sat across from this foreign man, who kept silent during my entrance into the lodge. When I settled into my seat on the ground, he spoke.

"I hear you started trading for the Charrucans," he said in fluent Mendican. "You exchanged with this here tribe last autumn?"

"I did. They made a very generous trade."

He pointed to the thin hide I had draped around my lower body. "That skin you're wearing," he said, "it's local to these parts. Anybody from around here could catch and kill to provide that."

"Yes, I got it from the Cavoques on the island," I said. Owing to his linguistic fluency, I assumed he had been exposed enough to this region to know which island I meant.

"Fitting," he said. I could sense a contained frustration. "I'm sure you've seen the hides owned by this tribe. You might even be hesitant to ask for some of them, given their quality."

I nodded. "They're very nice, much like yours." I motioned to his.

"They're exactly like mine," he said. "They're buffalo hides, and I gave them to the Mendicans." He paused, though not long enough for me to respond. "I also gave them some of the deer hides you bartered for last year; you'll notice a few of them are thicker and darker than your local breed."

"Indeed," I said, almost without considering whether I actually knew the difference.

The North Merchant continued. "I have a very intricate relationship in this region. My people elected me to be their tradesman; it is not an easy task. I am separated from my family for several months each year. The need to return to them limits how much I accomplish in a season." He nodded to the stack of hides that was further behind him, and I couldn't help but wonder how difficult it was for him to carry these goods. "The Charrucans modeled your role after my own," he said. "Except I know your kind. I've seen you men do things that disgust me. I don't know you, but I know you don't have the same life holding you back that I do. You need to tread carefully, Don Alvar."

"Are you threatening me?" I asked.

"Yes," he said. "Don't mistake this open land for an empty one. You're unbalancing a system that's been carefully laid over the course of many years."

"I didn't choose this role for myself," I said. "The Charrucans asked me to. They know what they're doing."

He shook his head. "There are more interests at stake than just the Charrucans'. You are a major advantage for them: a man without other responsibilities."

"I understand. You don't want me to upset your task, and I can respect that. But what would make this situation fair for you? I have a job to do, too, whether it seems to benefit you or not." I glared confidently into the North Merchant's eyes.

He nodded as if my gaze did not affect him. "I'm not trying to hurt the Charrucans. I just can't have you trading my hides across the region. You'll end up taking some of what my people need in return." Even while seated, the North Merchant was quite imposing. "Stick to trading your shells," he said. "I don't want my hides moving through your hands. I will provide these people with their warmth, Don Alvar, and you will provide them their tools."

"Understood," I said. "Any hide I'm given will remain with the Charrucans."

Though I found the prospect of limitations irritating, I did not want to upset a world I had yet to become fully familiar with. Toppling systems with an army was one matter, but doing so alone was an entirely different undertaking. But did I even want to upend this world around me? Perhaps the enjoyment of my new role deterred me from asserting myself.

Nevertheless, the North Merchant's threats did not sit well with me; when he left me in peace, I felt a determination to loosen his dominant grip. If I could find a way to take his role for myself, then I gladly would. The North Merchant was to be the gulf's most respected tradesman no longer.

CHAPTER 10

Argued Destination

———

ALONSO DEL CASTILLO

The Texas Mainland, 1531

Our group of twelve companions hastily fled the soured situation with the Cavoques.

Over a year, we traveled perhaps a total of sixty leagues—crossing the rivers, inlets, and bays which spanned the coastline. It was very troublesome to go anywhere. At one point, an enormous bay bent so far inland that it might have been suicide to try and walk around it; we eventually spent a great deal of strength building a raft from the meager materials available. Making it durable would have taken even more effort, so the twelve of us simply loaded ourselves on and took off for the other shore. The bay waters ended up being rough, rougher than anyone expected; the raft split, as we should have figured, killing one man from impact and forcing us to swim the remainder of the way. Each man focused on his own survival, and the stronger swimmers prevailed. Strong tides made three more Spaniards drown from their utter exhaustion. Diego Dorantes had initially dubbed it the Bay of the Holy Ghost, and I had never heard a poorer name for such an obstacle.

More rivers lay before us, as well as another inlet, but the air felt crisp, forcing us to remain through the winter. Misery ensued. Nothing covered our bodies, and the fires never warmed us from our initial swim; the whole time we survived off craw-fish and meadow grass pulled straight from the ground. Another man fell from a bad case of hypothermia. His passing marked five of our company dead, the other seven ready for the spring to arrive.

The rivers indeed grew warm enough to cross by springtime. It proved to be a simpler task compared to all we had gone through. We swam across another inlet, finally reaching the cove which seemed our last obstacle.

A native was standing there in the cove, not hostile in any way; Andrés Dorantes and I agreed we had seen him from somewhere before. I thought it looked out of place for his kind of indígena to live in such a remote spot. He had reeds piercing his chest, like the natives of the island, but I knew other tribes did the same all along the coastline. His face brightened as he approached, and he started shouting out words in Castilian. It shocked me, but I at once reasoned his connection to some long-lost segment of our expedition; no other explanation made sense.

He took us around the bend, where I saw a Spaniard tending to the fire. He cried out in joy when he noticed our arrival.

"God!" he said. "I can't believe it!"

The Spaniard said he was Figueroa, who we had sent ahead from the island a couple years ago. Figueroa was the last one alive; even his initial native guides had perished. We talked with him for hours, and he recounted the haunting deaths of the Governor, the Friar, and both their crews: all of it had been told to him by a man named Esquivel.

Figueroa led our pack nearer to what he called the Guaycones territory. Earlier that year, he and his fellow guides had suffered there at the hands of a tribe called the Marianes. He had vowed to never see those indígenas again, and wanted to escape any possibility of encountering them in the west. We in turn promised to avoid their camp.

Figueroa shook his head. "I don't think you understand," he said. "The natives out here aren't like those back toward La Florida. They're all spread out around the territory, and you never know when you're going to find them."

I shrugged, still moving forward. "We need to cross this territory either way. There must be a route which avoids most of the trouble."

"Not one which gets us any closer," Figueroa said. "Our whole goal is Nueva España, and I've started believing it's somewhere along the coast close by." Figueroa looked longingly down the gulf horizon.

"Close by?" I asked, somewhat sarcastically. "We've just gone along the coastline for two hundred miles, and nothing is here."

Figueroa's face became taut like a hound. "I've been walking around for two years, Captain, and I haven't gotten a single whiff of it being where we were told." He pointed westward, to the territories ahead. "But I'm guessing that's not going to matter to you much."

In all honesty, it didn't. "I respect what you've been through, Figueroa," I said, "but I don't agree with your thinking."

Figueroa chuckled. "Well, let's hear what the others have to say. Maybe they'll be more reasonable." Figueroa turned his gaze to Andrés Dorantes, and my co-captain nodded in reflection.

"Yes, this is something to discuss," Andrés said. "Figueroa, do you mind if I talk this over with my fellow captain for a moment?"

"By all means," Figueroa said. Taking the opportunity to rest from our trek, he reclined against a boulder. Andrés then approached me, and we stepped a few paces aside; his brother Diego, interested enough in our progress, decided to join.

"So, what do you think about all this, Andrés?" I asked.

"I think we need to get home," he said. "That is our first priority. We've all heard Nueva España to be due west from La Florida; there's no reason to believe Figueroa's southerly instincts are right. I say we continue into the Guaycones territory and get home faster."

"Great! I agree," I said.

Diego interjected. "Why are we going off of what we've heard before? 'Head due west' was the Governor's strategy; but now we know he's dead. What if Figueroa is right to look in other places?"

"Figueroa simply ran into trouble and wants to avoid it," Andrés, the brighter-haired Dorantes, said. "He's found nothing substantial to suggest we shouldn't go west. He just wants an out from future hostility."

Diego rolled his eyes. "That hostility could just as easily ruin us! Besides, we already have a sense for what's that way. Wouldn't it be more exciting to head along the coast and discover new territory?"

Andrés raised his voice. "Diego! Are you not aware of everything we've been through? You want to 'discover' more when we can barely find our next meal?"

Diego stared resiliently at his older brother. "Didn't we come here to explore? We came to seek out the best place in La Florida and to claim it as a Spanish territory. But the Governor's dead and we're continuing his cowardly retreat anyway. We're shriveling up when we could be making history."

I stayed quiet. Andrés breathed in and answered calmly. "I am your captain, Diego. I have good reason to believe our best move is due west. We need to get home; seven men cannot claim a Spanish territory. I will be parting with Figueroa and heading toward the Guaycones; since Estevanico is owned under my name, he will inevitably be joining me. My hope is for you to join us as well."

Andrés brazenly held his younger brother's green gaze; Diego slowly acquiesced.

"Understood," he said. "I'll head west with you, Andrés. I'd rather take a less enjoyable path than split up."

Andrés Dorantes smiled. "I'm glad you're coming." He turned to me. "I assume you are too, Castillo?"

I cleared my throat. "Like I said before, I don't agree with Figueroa. We should take the best-known route home."

The Dorantes brothers nodded and we disbanded our circle. After talking to our other companions, three were on board with the decision. I still needed to hear from the half-Basque missionary, however. I caught sight of him standing beside our old guide Figueroa.

"Asturiano has agreed to come with me," Figueroa said, standing up from against the boulder. "He sees the sense in following a man who's been out here for two years. How about you all?"

"The other men think like I do," I said, hiding my displeasure at Asturiano's decision. "We'll be taking the easiest route through the Guaycones territory."

Figueroa shrugged, and we managed to amicably part ways. The six of us heading west would never see him or the half-Basque missionary again.

CHAPTER 11

Restraints

—

ALVAR NÚÑEZ

Texas, October 1531

The eldest Charrucan leader was old enough to possess seniority, but young enough to not be ignored as senile. He spoke with me jovially about the rest of the trading season.

"I heard word of the Cavoques islanders," he said. "They had trouble this season, in the oyster beds here on the mainland." He clenched his teeth together. "Not very much was caught; not enough food. But the good news is they need what we've collected. They want hides for warmth, and you have a great number of them from the Mendicans, Don Alvar. We'll be making a trade for some household items. Not that we need them greatly; this is mostly charity." He gave himself a proud smile.

"Will I be leaving for the island then?" I asked, somewhat hesitant.

"Yes, we will boat you over to them." The elder's mind wandered for a moment as he stared at the lodge's roof.

I nodded. "Alright, but I need to avoid the Han."

"No, we avoid no one," he said firmly. "They now know you are one of ours."

Feeling assured by his comment, I put the hides in my sack; most were local, though a few felt slightly thicker. The more time I had spent trading, the more familiar I had become with the different tribes and interests at stake. The North Merchant's threat still loomed over me; however, if I ever planned to usurp his position, there was no reason to limit myself from bartering his hides. Besides, the Cavoques needed warmth.

I walked to the village center, where a couple natives stood waiting to leave; they looked tired in the early morning.

We all boarded the canoes. "The Cavoques are an awful people," one indígena said. "I've never enjoyed their company."

"I've met them," I said, helping row off from the shore. "But they never gave me trouble personally."

The indígena squinted his eyes as water splashed from his oar. "They keep the Christians there," he said. "They don't let them leave the island, even when they go to pick mainland oysters. They're a cruel people."

I stopped rowing, stunned by what he said. "Christians? What do you mean by that?" Perhaps the Charrucans were less up-to-date than I had thought if they still believed my friends were on the island.

"Two Christians are told to stay... all because the Cavoques are cruel."

I nearly shouted. "They still have two Spaniards on the island?"

He nodded without changing his expression. "Yes, they told us some Christians did not escape with the others."

"My God..." I muttered to myself. I immediately thought of the story of Lope de Oviedo not being able to swim; perhaps he was lingering there with another Spaniard.

The Charrucan rower's oars dipped into the cooling gulf water, but my mind could not get my hands to row in turn. "Keep rowing, Don Alvar," he finally said. I complied.

When our canoe landed, I did not delay in finding the two "Christians" I had been told of. I rushed toward a middle-aged woman in the camp to ask where the Spaniards were living; she pointed me to a hut on the outskirts of the village, well away from the rest of the tribe. Without consulting my Charrucan companions, I ran there.

Sure enough, I found two Spaniards, one kneeling over the other as he tended to a festering wound. I recognized both men. Lope de Oviedo seemed fine, although famished, and it appeared the notary, Jerónimo, had fallen ill with infection. Lope turned his head when he heard me enter.

"Captain Núñez," he said, almost whispering. His eyes widened with shock. "I thought you were dead."

My legs shook from the weighty hides on my shoulders. "I didn't know you were still here."

Lope looked ashamed. "We weren't able to swim across the water. They had to leave us here." His embarrassing story was indeed proven true once again.

"How come you haven't fled while picking oysters on the mainland?" I asked.

Lope motioned to his companion. The notary did not have the strength to talk, but he saw me well enough to know that I had arrived. "I couldn't leave him," Lope said. "Plus, the Cavoques won't give us the chance, not after the others managed to flee. They still want retribution for the food we ate during the hurricanes."

I nodded in understanding. "I wish it could be easier to take him."

Lope chuckled mildly, and I could see he was not planning to leave his sick friend; the young Spaniard had aged a decade in a couple short years. Though part of me wanted to, I decided not to leave toward the other survivors without at least giving Lope a fair warning. And as long as the notary was alive, I could assume the young man would remain. My role as tradesman would have to continue until Lope was ready.

"I'll be back, Lope." I left him, then gave the North Merchant's hides to the islanders before departing.

Summer 1532 arrived, and I had found a passion for my role. Tribes began to anticipate my visits more often, as if I were suddenly a fixture in their lives; oddly, they were becoming a fixture in mine.

One such tribe, the Deaguanes, lived a straight shot away from the natives of the wood. I had seen them the year prior to trade for flint, glue, and hard reeds; these made arrowheads and could be attached to finished arrows. The Deaguanes always needed shells to open the tough casing of mesquite beans. Every tribe this far west kept an abundance of mesquite. Mesquite was vital to these natives, in everything from healing to celebrations; however, I quickly learned that my best business lay with those who mostly needed my shells to eat.

The Deaguanes lived in a vast plain and had a tribal chief much like the Han. He welcomed me warmly, with a river-fish set before my place at his massive table. Though it was evening, the chief didn't wear any clothes over his chest.

"It is so good to have you here again," he said, speaking fluently in the tongue of the Charruco.

I knew a fair deal of Deaguanes, certainly enough to make these trades. However, the chief speaking a language not his own, the one I knew best, felt like a great sign of respect. I chose to make him feel important in return.

"I heard you needed shells," I said in his Deaguanes. "I came at once."

"You are quite the blessing; my people don't know what to make of it, a foreign man making our lives so much easier." Chief Deaguanes wore a large grin. "The women are always wondering about you too. 'Does he have a wife?' they always ask." He raised his eyebrows at me and chuckled. "I laugh at them; they all want to be married to you someday. But they have no idea how busy you are, with business leading you everywhere!"

All I could do was smile. "Marriage wouldn't be conducive." I might have elaborated on my married life in Spain, but it bothered me to think of my old life in comparison to this one. Did my success among these natives amount to anything in the grand scheme?

"No, it wouldn't," the chief said, suddenly dropping his playful tone. "Okay... Let's make the trade."

Chief Deaguanes exchanged with me outside the lodge, where I gave him nearly all my shells for his arrow-making materials. He also gave me an already completed arrow, kindly saying it was for my personal use. He offered I stay in his lodge that night, and since it was almost dark I accepted. The lodge was at the village's edge, and when we entered, the room was unexpectedly inviting; there were several younger women lying on the mats, and I wondered if this was their typical home.

"You must try some of this smoke," Chief Deaguanes said. "It relaxes you like nothing else." He sucked in a gray smoke from his pipe, filling his hanging belly with an unnatural air. "Go ahead and try some," he said.

He handed me his pipe and I examined it. This was unusual hospitality: a pipe and the presence of his people's most beautiful women. I felt a weird discomfort in my stomach at the thought. I both dreaded and hoped that this was his version of a brothel. But I put those thoughts aside.

I sipped in some smoke. Almost immediately I felt a scratch in my throat, but an unspeakable ease in my head came shortly after; the air around me was no longer bleak, and the trivial needs of thirst and hunger were lost in the moment.

I looked around at the women in the lodge, and for the first time in a while I was reminded of how my former priorities used to be desire instead of survival. The women were gorgeous; they beckoned me to join them, at least it seemed.

The chief laughed. "Go ahead! They'll love you."

My head spun. I wanted to ask *Who are they?* but the words did not leave my lips. Did they have husbands? I knew many wives were from other tribes; were they foreigners, too? Why did they live with the chief? The questions lingered, but I eventually pushed them away. I lay down, unsure of my current doings. I felt a woman's bare chest against me; I looked at her face and realized I had forgotten María's for good. Pleasure had never felt so simple. I finally felt desired again.

Perhaps I'd be punished, I thought in the days to follow. Perhaps I would get the same sores that befell the other men, those who had raped in Apalache. But I had not taken a woman forcefully. This was different. The chief had invited me in.

Of the week I spent in the Deaguanes village, I remember only one other event clearly. A man was horribly wounded by an arrow that had planted into his chest; his best friend mistakenly shot him on their morning hunt. I had spent the day in the smoking chief's lodge when I heard the news. The people around me were all in a panic, and it distressed me greatly. Hoping to calm the Deaguanes, and with some stroke of confidence, I volunteered myself to save his life. The tribe gathered around me as I wielded a large stone knife with which to cut the shaft. I did not think. I incised the man at such an angle that the arrow dislodged. A Deaguanes woman quickly pushed me aside to examine his chest, but found no sign that my cut had damaged him further. She cleaned the wound and I quickly felt relieved. People approached me asking what

I had done; I did not know how to answer them, though I accepted their gratitude regardless. On any different day my surgery might have killed him. Whether God or the smoke had guided my hand, I had no clue. Before they could ask anything more of me, I left the Deaguanes.

CHAPTER 12

Barrier to Entry

ALVAR NÚÑEZ

Texas, November 1532

Despite having little to trade with, I did not yet feel like returning to the natives of the wood. So I went further inland, toward the region of the Mendicans, which was a couple days walk away. The entire trek seemed to be through an open field of grass blades; no one tended to a crop in this empty section, and I rarely saw a person travel outside their distant home. I felt dreadfully exposed in the open space, first to the day's humidity and then to the evening's wind, since I wore nothing but my small deerskin; I knew I had no other choice but to endure.

After one such day of near-silent traveling, the beat of my footsteps brought me into a vast, natural arena where I stopped to rest. I reclined against the barren ground. Like a blanket, I placed the sack of various goods over my upper body. Sleep never came easily to me when no one else was around, so I laid there awake well into the night.

An owl's cry rang from a distance; crickets chirped, a nearby rodent scurried, and the peaceful hum of a dragonfly reached my ears. I started to fall into a lonely sleep.

Soon I heard it, however. The grass quietly crunched against a pair of feet as they crept toward me. I opened my eyes, remaining still.

A figure moved through the open plain, nothing blocking him from my sight. He didn't seem to care if I noticed.

I needed to get a better look. I slowly dragged the sack off my stomach, putting my body's weight against my hands so I could rise; tired arms lifted my upper half off the ground. Leaning over my legs until I was crouched into a ball, I tilted my head back to discern the approaching figure. The man was tall, brawny, and wrapped in a thick, dark hide. The North Merchant had come to confront me.

I reached my hand into the sack of goods, hoping to grab the finished arrow sitting near the top. The point felt dull, and the shaft looked weak, but it was the only defense I had. I yanked the arrow out from the bag.

My feet took off into a desperate sprint across the plain. The North Merchant held a spear in his right hand. Though he had been watching me, he did not expect my immediate rush. He lowered his weight, bringing his spear at head level; but I was already upon him.

I leapt at the large Northerner from the side, reaching across his chest to stab at the right shoulder. The Merchant dropped his spear with a painful cry. He was hardly subdued, however, and he threw me to the ground. His first blow landed in my rib, but I recovered, then engaged him in a brutal fight. My arrow had landed near his collar bone. Blood dotted his buffalo hide.

I jammed my fingers into the gash left by my arrowhead. He yelled. Wedging my hand between his wound and the shaped stone, I managed to free my arrow from the North Merchant's shoulder. I stabbed it into the same spot of the rib where he had struck. This allowed me to toss him over and kneel on top of him.

I shouted. "Why'd you follow me?"

He cried out. "You broke your word," he said. "I can't let you ruin my home."

I smashed my fist into the North Merchant's teeth. He stopped trying to hit back.

I leaned over him a while longer, not confident I had bested the man. A short observance of the North Merchant, however, made clear the gravity of his wounds. The tradesman was due to die.

Had he really tracked me because of what I gave the islanders?

I debated for several minutes how to handle his circumstance. He bled profusely, enough to fully darken his beloved hide. I shouted at him, and he didn't respond. If I were to attempt to save him, blocking his wounds, there would still be no hope for his survival. The field he had chosen for the attack was nowhere near a village.

Slowly, I sauntered off of him. I was exhausted, but to leave him between life and the grave would have been cruel.

Instead of my arrow, I used his spear.

The North Merchant made no sound when I took his life. I wondered, if given the choice, whether he would have prolonged death to deny me the reigns of his fate. *But what of my fate?* I dreaded the possibility that this encounter could spoil my arrangement with the Charrucans. I very much appreciated the respect and privilege owed to a tradesman. Without the North Merchant, I was now the most respected of them all. His life loomed over me no longer; only the burden of his death remained.

The night had grown colder, and I was weak. I walked several miles away; his buffalo hide in my hand. I needed the warmth it provided.

PART TWO

CONVERSO

CHAPTER 13

Inheritance

***

ANDRÉS DORANTES

Béjar, Spain, 1525...Three years before arrival in La Florida

---

My father's land was what many would call humble in size. It sloped ever so gradually against the green hill upon which his house was set. Despite spanning only the length of this single hill, his plot was meticulously maintained; every segment produced twice as much harvest as it did for his larger neighbors. Upkeep was a glorified endeavor, and it made for both a tiresome and enviable land to be raised on.

I sat by my father, Pablo, while he lay in bed. A pillow supported his head against the wall; he looked snug, like he could remain there for years without minding. The Spanish sun beat lovingly on Béjar, for the town and its surroundings lay right in the middle of the Iberian Peninsula. Distance from any coastline or sea-breeze made the sun's behavior an important force. Pablo had woven his life around its patterns. The sun guided when he rose, how he labored, and where he placed his home. Pablo's room by far received the most of this sunlight, and it was in this way that he kept life's warmth continual.

"I thought you were heading into town today," he said. He had my same deep tenor.

"I was. But I needed to attend to something here first." I shifted in his rickety bedroom chair.

"Really?" My dad smiled. "You wanted to check on the grapevines again?"

"No, it's out of season, Dad. And we have Estevanico for that anyway."

His smile dropped. "It's never stopped you from helping before."

I too was not smiling. "Well, that was when I thought this place would be passed down naturally," I said. "Now I know you're ripping it out from under me."

Pablo Dorantes nodded knowingly. Blue tile spanned the wall behind him, but only on its lower half; Pablo had called off the tiling project before its completion. "Ah, so that's why you stayed today," he said. "You 'need to attend' to disputing what I've set up."

"Yes, I do. It's ridiculous. And unfair."

"Unfair how?" The grayed man hardly moved a muscle as he spoke.

"You only have two real things to give us, Dad: Estevanico and your estate. I love this piece of land more than anything, and you know Diego couldn't care less for it." I tried to maintain some sense of calm. "You also know how close Diego is to the *morisco*. We may find their friendship unnerving, but they are the same age; they've grown up together. The right choice is obvious. He wants Estevanico; I want the land. But you've given us the reverse."

My father soaked in my words for a moment, then carefully lifted himself more upright against the wall. He faced me sternly. "I'm not giving Diego the land. I'm not a fool... I know you two would trade your lots the moment I die."

My brow raised. This was news to me. "What's he getting then? Your money?"

"No, Diego's getting the benefits that'll come when the land gets sold. As will you. The day I die, this house and field are going to our neighbor Salvador. He's then paying a good sum to the banker from Sanlúcar. That banker will have orders to wait until there's a respected expedition where at least one of you can enter with rank. He'll have your three tickets, and the rest of my money is to keep you living in an apartment until he finds what I've asked."

I bent forward in my chair, blowing out a short, frustrated sigh. "Dad... you can't be serious. You're going to give away our home to finance Diego's stupid dream? Have you lost your mind? There's no reason for this; it's cruel."

"There is a reason, Andrés."

"Oh, I'd love to hear it!" I chuckled nervously. "You know, there's nothing to stop me from changing this. I can go tell Salvador that I'm keeping the land, and I'll find the banker to let him know he won't be taking the vacation he wanted. Our money's staying in this estate."

"You're mistaken, Andrés. Salvador knows to respect a man's will, as does every man who was raised right. I'm starting to doubt the job I did with you." My father let this sink in. "I won't take criticism from my own son in the last months of my life. So you'll listen to what I have to say, Andrés, and you'll listen well."

"Alright." I leaned back in my chair, defeated.

Pablo cleared his throat. "I figured you might try to sell Estevanico; or more likely, set him free. But selling him won't afford you more than some rent; and if he's set free, they'll ship him back to the Moors. Or maybe they'll do worse: his conversion isn't as believable as he thinks." A light shone through in my father's eyes as he began to reminisce. "Estevanico was always my war prisoner. I spent my whole youth fighting to get the Muslims out of Iberia; now, we're no longer under their control, and he's under mine. It's justice. I suggest you maintain this justice; it's why he's getting passage with you and your brother."

I shrugged. "I don't have much of a choice it seems. Even though you've said he's my inheritance."

Pablo ignored me and gave a slight chuckle. "I had an opportunity to do the same, you know. The very year we pushed the Muslims out, Cristóbal Colón was recruiting the best men who had served. I was offered a position. I could've gone. But instead I hunkered down and chose to retreat into the home I'd fought to reconquer." My father shook his head to himself. "I should've gone, Andrés. I was young, and I chose the life of an old man."

"But it worked out," I said. "You met mom."

"No, I should've waited to meet her. I missed the greatest opportunity of my generation; another few years, and I might have brought her with me into the new frontier."

"Dad, that's a pointless regret." My tone had moved from anger to reassurance. "You could just as easily have died."

"Ah, but what's one death compared to the other?" he said. "I will say, at least with this one, you two were born. The opportunity is still open. You're both young; you can make the choice I declined."

I spoke softly. "It's not making a choice, Dad, when you've forced me into it."

"You'll thank me," he said. "It'll pay off more than either of us can know." My father reclined further into his bed. "Do you see that knife on the table, Andrés?"

I looked over. It was the same knife which never seemed to leave his side. "Yes, Dad, you've told me about it many times."

"It's yours now," he said.

"Really?" I never imagined he would part with it. For all my anger at the rest of his will, receiving his beloved relic made me glad. "Thank you, Dad. Truly."

"Let it be a reminder," he said, almost ignoring my gratitude, "that you need to take this path as your own, Andrés. An expedition will be able to sniff out who's hungry and who came because they had to. Diego could get promoted over you. Imagine how embarrassed you would be, under your little brother's command. You best act like you're hungry."

My mood dropped once more, and I felt like life was out of my control.

Pablo smiled and drifted off. The Spanish sun still beat against his face as he rested.

CHAPTER 14

Prickly Pear Season

ANDRÉS DORANTES

Texas, April 1532...Four years after arrival in La Florida

So far, our old guide Figueroa had been proven wrong. The western natives he warned us of had not only welcomed us, but had also agreed to help determine our path forward. The Guaycones, as they went by, only needed a couple weeks to ensure our safety among the tribes ahead; with a convincing word, they could make our journey home both quick and comfortable. In the meantime, we would work for them as compensation. I dreamed consistently of returning to Spain, so this arrangement did not bother me in the slightest. I desperately wanted to be in a land I could comprehend.

The Guaycones, as it happens, were not an easy people to comprehend. Their words sounded very different when compared to the eastern tribes, and they lived over a more spread-out area than anyone I had met. A few of them guided our company of six nearly a dozen miles to their territory's northernmost outskirts, where the tribe was able to grow beans and some other crops. Unfortunately, these yields were not abundant, since the farms stood so close to the Marianes territory, with whom the Guaycones often disputed. The huts on this land were scarce and uninviting. The wind kept an arid warmth, but heat thankfully distracted me and the others much less than the cold; we six had all been raised in some form of hot weather and otherwise lacked proper clothing.

The Guaycones told us to stay in a hut right next to the fields, saying we might only be there for a little while. For two days, they left us alone without coming to the hut for any reason; we weren't brought any food or water, so it prompted me to try hunting a shrew for its meat. I did not succeed. At the dawn of the third day, however, several natives barged into the hut, pulling everyone to their feet and yelling, "It's time to farm!" Exhausted, we complied.

Their plants already seemed to have failed beyond the point of recovery. I think the Guaycones knew it, but they left a single jar of muddy water on the ground anyway and beckoned us to get to work. "What do we even do?" my younger brother asked me.

"All we can do is water them," I said, shrugging.

Diego chuckled. "Yeah, with mud." He was not far off. We spent the day pouring small amounts of mud onto each plant, spreading out the contents of the single jar. Barberries should have been growing off the red-tipped bushes. However, where the bush-bases were supposed to be a lively green, they were instead a stifling brown. I felt my stomach churn at the sight.

The next ten mornings brought with them the same work; everyday, the plants looked worse, and I grew more emaciated. Overall hunger forced us to consider a departure. Diego spoke up. "Let's get out of here while we have the energy," he said.

I firmly responded. "No. We don't know enough about this region to make it far. We should bide our time until Chief Guaycones can deliver on his promise." Diego was unsettled with my decision. But as the others all agreed to stay, he too submitted.

My instinct was quickly proven wrong. In the middle of the night, a group of Guaycones awoke us by dragging us up from our beards; mine had grown so thick, long, and tangled that this motion yanked out clumps of hair. It was immeasurably painful. They cuffed my arms with a tight rope and shoved me out of the hut. The same was done to the others. We were told to stay on the ground until morning.

Diego sat near me on the dirt; his demeanor had retreated to that of a broken child. He was slouched over, and his green eyes had lost their brightness. "I'm sorry I brought you here."

"It's not for you to be sorry," I said, leaning against the tightly-thatched wall's exterior. "This was the route I convinced you to take."

"No, I mean for this expedition in general. Exploring is what I wanted, not you. Dad sent us here for my sake." My younger brother frowned. He had the same sulking face our mother once did. "Making my mark mattered more than anything; I never once thought we'd be ruined like this. We'll be lucky just to survive."

"Yes, and we've been lucky this far." I gave my brother a comforting shoulder nudge. "There are only six survivors, Diego, and we two brothers and our Moor make up half of them. Sounds to me like we're not meant to die." My words were nothing but a reassurance, and I think he realized as much; he knew how badly I wished to return home.

"Just forgive me when you end up feeling angry, Andrés," Diego said. "And Dad, too. Please don't hold this against us."

I faked a smile. "I wasn't planning on it." I turned away from him and fell asleep.

My co-captain Castillo and I soon determined to speak with the Guaycones chief, both about our treatment and the failing crops. Diego, in true fashion, chose to come along with us. He brought Estevanico with him.

The chief's dwelling spanned a less impressive size than the lodges in La Florida, although it was noticeably better sealed by dried mud. Chief Guaycones sat tall in his wooden chair, a man in much stronger physical condition than most his age. The four of us stood before him solemnly.

"Your crop is failing," Castillo said in the Deaguanes tongue, which we all spoke to a certain degree. We had briefly stayed with the Deaguanes to learn their widely-spoken phrases. "We're concerned, both for our sake and for your own."

"Don't be worried." The chief did not speak in the Deaguanes he'd been addressed in; after only these couple weeks, he expected us to follow along in his native Guaycones. "We leave for the prickly pears in the summer. You'll be coming with us."

I wanted to make sure I had heard him correctly. "Coming with you?"

"Yes," he said. "I lied to you before. You won't be moving forward."

My mood abruptly sank, as did the faces of my companions. Dreams of a smooth journey home had been dashed.

"You're no better than a slave driver!" Diego was never one to contain his emotions. He shouted in Deaguanes. "You might think you have all the power here, but this isn't your domain. We're not too far from Nueva España; the Spaniards know to look for us, and they won't like what they find."

"Don't act so blameless," the chief said. He now spoke the tongue we knew better, wanting his words to be fully comprehended. "You are all connected to the men from the South. I've heard the things they do. Every man with sense knows to show your kind no mercy; we must band together to keep you out. The conquering Aztecas never reached us, and the foreigners who replaced them won't either." He looked strongly at Diego. "I'll remember your threat to me. I won't remember it kindly."

At these words, I saw what looked like a slight grin on Estevanico's face; it made me feel sick inside. My late father's slave was normally so reserved. Did he think this was funny?

Chief Guaycones immediately dismissed us from his home, then he ordered us to be separated into three different villages. Estevanico and Captain Castillo were placed at the territory's western edge, while my brother

Diego and the horseman Cháves were moved to the east; I was stuck in the middle of the northernmost village with a man named Valdivieso.

Months passed in separation and uncertainty. The same hard, fruitless labor filled my days. Each hour numbed my soul.

As summer approached, the entire tribe prepared to travel outside their territory. Collection of the cactus fruit called prickly pear was imminent. One Guaycones man bragged to me about the event. "Every tribe in the region spends these three months eating them," he said. "Our crop always fails, but the prickly pears never do. They grow in the same place each year, and we never miss them." He laughed. "Now you get to pick them for us!"

The prospect of migration was terrifying. Where exactly would we be taken? We might face added trouble finding our way home from there.

I strongly desired to escape, but the Guaycones had beaten my legs with a rod. Valdivieso asked if he could flee without me, and I gave him my blessing. How could I not? Keeping my fellow Spaniard in such miserable condition would be cruel, even if I was his captain.

The evening before the prickly pear migration, Valdivieso attempted his escape. He was promptly caught and brought back to the village. They beat him to death with the same rod.

I tried my best not to dream of the bloody incident, but it had completely replaced my dreams of home.

Morning came, and I was marched to the fields of the prickly pear. The tribe walked in high spirits, as if this were the year's greatest celebration; I felt quite far from this general mood. Limping ahead took all my strength. I felt so desperately alone.

Eventually, I spotted Castillo and Estevanico in the migrating fray. What a relief.

"Castillo!" I yelled.

He looked back. "Andrés!"

I finally caught up to him and my father's slave. "Are you alright?" I asked.

"We're alright," Castillo said. "But you: your legs look terrible. And, Valdivieso, is he...?"

"Yes." I avoided elaboration, and Castillo nodded somberly. Estevanico stood awkwardly to the side, allowing us the chance to speak but not engaging. I continued. "Have you seen my brother or Chavés?"

A Guaycones man heard me speak. Though he could not understand us, he inferred as to our topic and interrupted. "Are you looking for the over-talkative foreigners?" he asked me.

"I suppose so," I said.

The indí pointed out into the east, smiling. "See the smoke over there?"

There was indeed a smoke rising higher by the minute. Raging, large it grew, visible across the flat plain. A hut had clearly been set ablaze.

The season passed like a blur in my mind. My brother had followed his dreams to the grave.

Soon to leave the prickly pear fields, we three survivors planned our escape; before we could be separated again, Castillo and I took advantage of this last chance to deliberate. Nonetheless, my emotions were seared, and I lacked energy. I contributed little to our planning.

"Estevanico and I will go southwest as soon as we return," Castillo said. "There's a tribe known as the Yguaces that way. However, Andrés, that route is too dangerous to pursue from your hut, as you'd be passing through the most populated Guaycones village." He looked me very carefully in the eyes. "You'll need to cross over to the north, going toward a tribe called the Marianes. Estevanico and I will wait no longer than six months for you to meet us; this should give you time to account for winter and the logistics of reaching the Yguaces from there. If we don't see you by then, we'll have to move on. You understand all this?"

"I understand," I said. "Best of luck to you."

"You too, Andrés." Castillo gave a warm smile. "We'll see you soon."

Estevanico finally spoke. "Goodbye, Andrés."

"Goodbye, Estevanico," I said.

As soon as I returned to the Guaycones village, I immediately went through with the plan. I stole alone across the tribal border, quietly praying for an end to my loneliness.

CHAPTER 15

Crossing the Channel

ALVAR NÚÑEZ

March 1533

Swimming to the mainland proved a lot harder with someone clinging to my back. The brisk waves crashed against me as I struggled to finish each stroke. When the water came over my head and soaked my hair to where it seemed frozen, I felt like cannon fire had woken me from a peaceful sleep. I was scared to the bone, though only because my skin was useless protection; the layer I did wear, a fur coat with a gaping hole, provided me no warmth. It only added to the weight I carried.

Lope had been very hard to convince. He kept saying he might die if he tried to swim across, that I should go alone. I wouldn't hear it. So I carried him on my back like a child, and luckily the waves did not grow large enough to drown us.

When we arrived to shore, we headed straight for the Deaguanes. Lope nearly cried when he realized such generous natives lived not too far off all these years. "If only I left earlier," he said. "I could've been here instead." I remained in the Deaguanes camp for many nights, allowing the younger man to be at peace before we went into unknown territory.

"I will send you to the Quevenes," the plump Chief Deaguanes said. "I do not like or trust these people, but they will get you farther west than I ever could." I nodded in understanding, as I did not fear the Quevenes; I had met them before, but not enough times to be fully familiar. Perhaps there was a side to these natives I was not seeing clearly.

Lope and I smoked with the chief through the night. The morning came, and Lope kissed an indígena woman goodbye; he observed the camp with an already-nostalgic air. I urged the young man onward, and we set out across the plain.

Plains turned into forest, and forest into plains again. "Captain Núñez, wait." Lope gaped at the ground.

I stopped. "Yes?" I asked. "Lope, what are you doing?"

"We're making a mistake," he said. "Why are we leaving?"

I answered instinctively. "To find the other Spaniards. To get back home."

"But why?" Lope's face contorted earnestly. "I'm trying now, as we're walking closer to the others, but I can't think of a single reason why we should be going back home."

"Lope, you can't be serious," I said. "We're stranded out here. We failed to claim La Florida."

"I know. And how does going home help that?" Lope hardly looked my way; he seemed to be addressing himself. "Should we return just to venture out and fail again? Because I certainly don't want to have my old life back. I went on this expedition for a reason."

"So you're satisfied right now?" I asked. "If you are, that's fine. We can run back and tell Chief Deaguanes you'd like to spend the rest of your life smoking and sleeping with his women."

Lope shook his head, frustrated. "Núñez, you're not hearing me. What's the problem with this life? You yourself managed to become a well-liked merchant in this region. The same accomplishment would take a decade back in Spain."

He caught me off guard with this statement. I gathered a response. "But here, it's not the same... right? I mean, if I achieve something among the natives, does it even matter?"

Lope now looked directly at me. "It's better than achieving nothing somewhere else." I felt my stomach drop.

"Well, I didn't leave my merchant role on good terms anyway," I said. "I couldn't embrace this life even if I wanted to."

Lope slowly nodded. "Alright. I understand. It's just that I myself have no reason to go home. There's no one here to tell me what to do, and I think I'd rather stay."

I was about to acquiesce, but then I remembered the swim I had performed to bring him closer to home. "Easy for you to say, Lope. I had to drag you off the island; I risked my life for nothing."

"That wasn't for nothing," Lope said. "I thank you for it endlessly. But since I'm not in misery anymore, I can clearly see the right choice." He paused. "Would you like to stay here with me, Núñez?"

I answered instantly. "No. I'm heading toward the others. Have a safe journey east, Lope."

"And you as well, Núñez," he said. I parted ways with the young man.

Upon reflection, I realized my travels would be much easier without Lope dragging me back. I was happy to be rid of the burden.

Was being alone from Spanish company as bad as being truly alone? Within myself, I could not determine the answer.

A short Quevenes man eventually approached me near a riverbank; even I was taller than him. He seemed less interested in my presence than any native prior, which led me to believe he had been exposed to other Spaniards.

"Excuse me," I said in the common Deaguanes tongue. "Have you seen any foreigners like me?"

The short indí nodded. "I did not so long ago. They told me no more would be coming... but here you are."

"Do you know where they went?" I asked.

He laughed. "Yes, the western tribes talk all about them. They are with the Yguaces, and also the Marianes to the north. Those people brag whenever there is something new to tell."

I struggled to find the humor. "I see... Do they say how many there are?"

"Three of them. They have a habit of leaving to other tribes; however, my western neighbors make sure to punish this." The short man's face filled with a dramatic rage, simply to illustrate his story. "They are beaten, and kicked, and badly bruised with rods. The Guaycones would hit them the worst; they killed three other foreigners because it pleased them to watch."

I shuddered a little. "How can I reach the Yguaces and Marianes? I'm looking for my countrymen."

"You ask a lot of questions," the short indí said. "Those people live very spread out, even from their own villages. They are scarce because they often die from a lack of food; it would be hard to know where in those territories your foreigners are living. Nonetheless, I do know that the Marianes yearly come to this river, on the other shore, to search for walnuts. The time is arriving very soon."

"Thank you," I said. I tried to think of anything else I required. The river ahead of me looked daunting. "Do you happen to have a boat I can cross with?"

"I do. But such a gift would cost you."

His response was expected, but the only item I owned was the thick hide with the gaping hole. "In exchange for your boat, I will barter my enviable hide. This is a commodity you will not find anywhere near here; I can personally guarantee this."

The short indí's unusually round face beamed. "Oh really? Your hide sounds appealing, if only for the story it must hold; I'll make your trade."

I nodded, pleased. "You've been quite helpful. I thank you wholly." The short man helped me carry his canoe to the riverbed; we parted ways, then I boarded and rowed the canoe to the western bank. My naked body then traversed a well-trodden path around the thickets in the northernmost woods. For miles and days I went on. As long as I had water and food nearby, the pain of a trek no longer fazed me.

At the coastal woods' other end sat the Marianes' makeshift village. It was used solely during the walnut-picking season, I assumed. The indígenas moved about, picking from the Juglans trees wherever they could. There was an abundance to be gathered.

I soon spotted him, walking in my direction from the lodges. It was Captain Andrés Dorantes. The very same Dorantes who had not seen me in four years.

I yelled. "Andrés!"

His eyes turned white with fear. He stood there, frozen at the sight of me.

"I thought I'd never see you again," I said. I felt my eyes begin to well.

Dorantes came to his senses. "Me too," he said, pausing. "It's about time."

We examined each other for a moment before his comment made me burst into laughter. What he said hadn't been particularly funny, but the laughter kept me from crying. Dorantes soon flashed a big smile. He started laughing too, though tears fell down his face regardless. I joined him, letting out a sob while I laughed.

The two of us embraced each other as long-lost countrymen, united in cause. We were both shamefully exposed, but the years had drained away any natural shame in nakedness. I felt glad, satisfied to have found my fellow Spaniard; alongside this, however, I felt the loss of leaving something behind.

CHAPTER 16

Morisco

———

ESTEVANICO

Summer 1533

The plan had been in effect for nearly a year, but Alonso del Castillo and I were still stuck with the Yguaces. They treated us like beasts.

I knew how it felt to be treated like a beast, and it does not settle well with a man. The Yguaces liked to beat us and work us tremendously hard, and I imagined it would not take much for them to become murderers. But honestly, I knew this to be the same for any man. The Spaniards and the Portuguese had that tendency; even the Greeks were tempted to be abnormally mean-spirited. I had seen and heard of sickening violence throughout all of Europe and throughout Africa and Asia, whether it be from the Venetians, the Moors, the Slavs, or the Arabs: it does not make a difference where a man is from, because regardless, he will always harbor the hatred and innate evil that are commonly hidden inside everyone. So why be surprised by the cruelty of these indígenas?

When they burned Diego Dorantes alive, and killed the two others as well, I was not shocked. These were hostile foreigners who had been placed in front of them, albeit without their weapons or strength or will. The indígenas risked their humanity by committing such an act, much in the same way the Spaniards had given up theirs by slaughtering the native masses. Men often forget that their humanity is contingent on the choices they make. Whether they kill or strive for tranquility is all a reflection on their humanity. Yet when people are trapped, and stripped of their ability to make decisions, they are being stripped of human nature. This in itself is enslavement, the most aching form of torture, the kind I have suffered nearly my whole life.

My father was a goat herder, living in the hilly pastures of Azamor's eastern edge. Azamor was a harbor town, fortified and guarded on the Atlantic Coast of Morocco, leagues from a city the Spanish called Casablanca; but as one walked inland from the fortified harbor, a large set of hills dotted the countryside in all directions. Farmers and shepherds spent their days in these hills, doing their work without ever bothering to go into town; my father was among the herders, living on perhaps the largest hill within view of the ocean.

My father had six children, three girls and three boys. His first wife bore him a daughter, and then a son, then another daughter; when she died, he remarried, having another daughter, then me, and then my little brother. My father blamed the poor boy for my mother's death in child-birth, and afterward he found no point in remarrying. But still he enjoyed his life on that hill. I never had the chance to meet his eldest daughter. I did meet my half-brother, though, since he regularly visited and even moved back in with us once he found his wife. He was planning to join the infantry of our town, to fend off the enemies of our current war; despite his passionate spirit, my father managed to convince him that a life in goat herding had more purpose. My other half-sister married when I was very young, but I do remember her face and the very distinct way in which she spoke; my older sister, too, was soon to be married when I was perhaps nine or ten years old. It was in these months that her groom visited us as much as possible, always bringing gifts and presenting himself in the most mannerly fashion. My father approved of him, and so did I. He had been kind enough to give me a pair of his old sandals.

My younger brother had also received some kind gift, though I don't remember quite what it was; at the time, he was six and I was ten, and we rarely fought despite both being so similar to each other. We wanted to be fishermen, since we could always see the ocean from our hill; we rarely went out to it, however, and so each trip to the harbor caught our attention. But as my father aged, our trips became less frequent, and our desire to be fishermen only grew.

In the midst of my childhood, the Portuguese began to make good on their promise of coastal dominance.

Their plan at the time (and what I presume is still their plan) had been to travel by ship along the western coast of the African continent, venturing inland only to strip the country of its vital resources. They targeted only towns on the coast... Azamor was their next stop. It was not long until the Portuguese fleet made its entrance.

Everyone wept except my little brother and me. We were too young to know how awful it was, the burning of our town and the deaths of those around us; but once the soldiers made it over the hills to our cottage a few days later, my brother and I cried harder than we had since birth. My father was waiting for them, headstrong, despite my siblings and their spouses wanting to flee to the east. "We must leave!" they said, but my father insisted on defending his home. The couples still wished to run, but how can sons and daughters desert their father at his most desperate hour? So we all stayed on our hill and waited for the Portuguese.

First they slaughtered our goats, which left me debilitated. Every memory beyond that was a blur until I arrived at the harbor. The harbor, Azamor, which I had not been to in some time, was not the same place where my brother and I dreamed to sell fish. Its marketplace did not bustle, and the fishermen could not be seen from the shore. Why? Because the town had been properly set to flames, and the only visible ships were those of the Portuguese. Some of those ships housed their infantry and others housed their navy; but the ship I was bound for housed the chosen people of Azamor. No one else in my family had survived to join me.

They took my clothes, and the sandals that had been given to me, and then they tied my hands in front of my stomach. I got on the ship, still crying, far too upset to take in my surroundings, far too overwhelmed to cling to my freedom.

The man who bid the highest on me was a farmer from a town in the heart of Iberia. The region used to belong to my people, yet now my people were their property.

The man had two sons, and no wife anymore, with a few sheep and cattle. I never tried to run away, and I often pretended the two sons were like me and my little brother; I desperately wanted to leave, though I never showed my anger. If I ever were to try to flee, my life would be at the mercy of those in the countryside, who would surely give me a punishment worse than death.

The father, Pablo, looked very old, much like mine; but I had never called my dad *papá*, and these children never called their father *abba*. They had only one slave—me—to do their fieldwork. Pablo was too old to do it, and he rarely made his sons help me unless they were in trouble. Soon the family taught me their language, and soon they told me that I needed to apostatize and adopt a Catholic name; they explained that Christianity should be my faith if I were to go to heaven, that I needed to become a follower of God. "But I already believe in God," I said, and this made Pablo very angry.

"You are degrading His name by saying such a thing," he told me. "Your god is a sick and twisted one; how could he be the true God if you chose to pray to Muhammad instead of Christ and the Virgin Mother? There is so much to faith you do not understand, and you will not eat more than a morsel until you come to accept it."

For weeks I went without speaking to the farmer, and for a long time I felt trapped. Would dying for such seemingly trivial differences be worth it, especially with the promise of better treatment? Is apostasy really such a sin?

Soon they started calling me Estevanico, and whenever they congregated, I joined in their prayers; but my prayers in private were not the same, not spoken the same and not from the same heart. I prayed the prayers my father had taught me as a boy, though who they were for and why they were prayed I lost track of.

All I know is that my prayers were always prayed alone, and even still I am the sole man of my creed amidst a company of foreigners, all bearing the same hatred that every other man is known to possess. Now, however, these captors also bore my same burdens. I found it hard not to relish in their suffering. I felt no true sorrow when men like Diego died.

Andrés at last reached us when his Marianes came to visit the Yguaces tribe, who carried Castillo and myself. Alvar Núñez had also arrived. I wasn't expecting him, to say the least, since I had thought Núñez dead for a very long time; it almost felt like meeting a ghost.

It was the summer of 1533, the season of the prickly pear. The fruit had a great taste and a soothing texture, but eating too much left me dehydrated. Nevertheless, this was far better than the serpents, ant eggs, lizards, spiders, and salamanders the Yguaces ate most of the year; they even cooked the meat from poisonous vipers. Late summer brought the best opportunity for food, and so it was cause for every tribe to journey to the same location.

The prickly pears were their regional celebration; for me and the Spaniards, however, it was the only opportunity to meet and discuss. In hushed conversation, we four planned how to exact an escape. They three planned, rather, as I stood in silent observance.

"It has to be now," Castillo said. "We didn't expect, Andrés, that the Marianes also migrated here. And God, Alvar, that you were even alive, let alone able to find your way here. Having us all together right now feels like too special an opportunity; we need to take action." The other two men agreed; we would be leaving as soon as possible. Events precipitated, however, that made this decision impossible.

The Yguaces and the Marianes had been spending this recent time in quite friendly relations; they ate and celebrated together daily. About a week into this rare intermingling, a man from the Marianes complained that his wife continued to meet alone at night with a Yguaces man. The woman claimed she never said more than a few words to the other man, and that her husband made it up so he could beat her. It quickly became a very big issue among the entire population.

The Yguaces backed the woman, shaming the man for beating his wife; the Marianes, on the other hand, threw small rocks and wood at the supposed adulteress whenever she walked by. The entire tribal relationship fell apart. Chaos ensued; small acts of foul play and violence were daily being committed between the Yguaces and Marianes. We were caught in an unstable situation which could have advantaged our escape plan, if not for the unanticipated decision of the two tribes to depart to their territories. The Marianes walked far away from the Yguaces one morning, and Castillo lost all knowledge of his fellow Spaniards' whereabouts.

I was indifferent to the success or failure of our overall "return home." In native bondage, in Spanish bondage: what was the difference? Even based on appearance, they both viewed me as a foreign entity; I probably suffered harsher treatment because of it.

Castillo had a much different opinion, and over the next year I heard it expressed many times. "Should we run away now?" he would ask. "I wonder if Alvar and Andrés are already on their way ahead, or if they're waiting to see us in the next harvest season."

I usually shrugged in response; however, as the months dragged on, I began to feel bad for Castillo. His demeanor toward me, I gathered, was not of belittlement, but one of a scared child seeking advice. We would spend a day fanning flames to keep the mosquitoes away from the Yguaces village, or another day marveling at their cruel practice of abandoning infant daughters to die of exposure (the Yguaces only married women from other tribes, and thus saw their own women as future wives of the enemy). During these days, Castillo would annoy, frustrate, and over-engage me, but he would never bark specific orders or play into his perceived rank. I finally decided to ease his paranoia.

"We should stay, Castillo," I said. "Andrés is the most sedated with grief I have ever seen him; he will follow whatever Núñez says. And Núñez, undoubtedly, will want to wait for us. He has spent so long alone that his one hope is companionship. Bide your time, Castillo, and do not worry."

Castillo thanked me and we spent another half year under the rod, fending off mosquitoes and chasing deer.

CHAPTER 17

Escape

ALONSO DEL CASTILLO

Inland Texas, July 1534

Alvar Núñez approached us like an overworked dog during the prickly pear summer of 1534. Our two tribes were once again in the same region; we could once again speak.

"The war's ending," he said. A war had come about between the Yguaces and Marianes over the dispute from the previous year. Other tribes, most of them also visitors to the prickly pear fields, had joined in on this conflict; the war became a massive and brutal effort between two intertribal alliances. Now, apparently, it was coming to an end. "They are beginning peace talks tonight," Núñez said. "It could take some time, but I've heard it confirmed that they'll be trading me and Andrés to these distant tribes I've never even heard of. Who knows what the Yguaces are planning for you; we all make good bartering tools."

"So we need to leave right away," I said emphatically. "We'd better run before the war ends."

"Yes, of course. They plan to put whatever peace agreement in effect at the end of the summer." Núñez looked at the sky. "I've been watching the moon, trying to keep track of the months. Tonight should be a new moon. I will be here with Andrés, in this very spot, on the night of the full moon; I'll be leaving that night regardless of whether you are here. I hope you show up."

I wondered whether Estevanico would come with me to the meeting point. Here he was, a last survivor of a horribly doomed expedition, and yet he was under the enslavement of his fellow survivor. All he had to do was run; any direction, and Andrés Dorantes would never find him again. I watched the Moor all day, staring and wondering whether he would depart before we reunited with his master. There was this fight in his eyes, but it was covered in a glaze of pain and calm. Sure enough, Estevanico walked with me that night to where the full moon shone.

None of us greeted each other. We ran immediately.

The threat of the rising sun chased us in every respect. A step southwest was another length away from the heat and visibility of day; flatness consumed the plain, enough to expose us the moment the sun made its appearance. Fueled by nothing, we ran.

Smoke loomed up ahead. Smoke once meant possibility and the lure of gold. Smoke now meant life and the chance for hospitality or hardship.

The sun reached the sky before we reached the smoke. Had we run far enough away from potential pursuers? An internal knot weighed my center toward the ground, forcing my feet to land with heaviness. Sharp stings of pain wicked away the sweat that held my last supply of moisture. Even if smoke meant hardship, there would surely be water; whatever village lay ahead, I needed to make it there.

The sunlight allowed me to see an indígena's figure.

"Estevanico," Dorantes said. "Run up to him. Tell him we're friendly."

The Moroccan sprinted to the man ahead, hoping to catch his attention. By the time we other three reached their conversation, Estevanico had rummaged through every language he knew; the native didn't know Yguaces, which was the closest tongue. He did, however, respond in broken Marianes.

"I'm from the village right there," the indí said.

"Good, yes," Estevanico said, panting. "We want you to take us there. Can we come?"

"Yes," he said. "You should follow me. They'll want to know you're here."

I added another question. "What's your tribe called?"

"The Avavares," he said. "I just speak this Marianes when we're trading."

The indí led us to the village outskirts, where two guards stood without menace, though they each carried a bow. The guards spoke with the indí before deciding to let us through; the older one addressed us in his own broken Marianes. "We think we've heard of you," he said, "or about these foreigners who have done strange things to the east. You look like you would be them." This older guard smiled. "Our people will want to see you."

They'd want to see us? Why?

I hesitantly entered the village, which seemed saturated with huts. An Avavares woman approached us with water, and I drank my fill as I reclined in the hut of the village elders. I wholly hoped their hospitality was not another rouse to trap me into more enslavement. My fate rested in their hands.

A gathering of Avavares leaders introduced themselves as I eerily regained my strength. "We pride ourselves on being the closest people to the prickly pears," one elder said. "We Avavares have held this position for generations, and it has given us several advantages. There are deer here, and from them we make the strongest bows in the region: the Northern peoples trade us lots of buffalo hides and meat for these bows every year. This is how we all know Marianes, which is the tongue we speak to guarantee access to trade; the northern peoples can only learn so many languages, you know." The elder laughed, and his colleagues joined him for a moment. His smile soon faded, however. "All this has changed, you see, since the northern merchant died and the wars started. It's a good thing we are near the prickly pears. We are lucky to be the best tribe at finding and preparing them." The entire room gave their assent, with some even cheering. "We'll be bringing you some of our fruit shortly; but unfortunately you'll never get to try its powder on the northern buffalo meat. That was always my favorite meal."

The elder's word soon came true. Avavares women brought in their version of a prickly pear dish, and I could not have been more relieved by its appearance. They explained their whole preparation process as I ate: first, they removed the cactus covering. This covering was pulverized into a powder for later use. Then, knowing that the inner fruit caused dehydration, the Avavares squeezed out its refreshing juice into whatever jars they owned. If they ran out of clay jars, then they would dig nearby pits to temporarily store the juice. The main dish, therefore, was a squeezed prickly pear fruit topped in its own powder, typically served alongside some juice and venison. I thanked the women for what was easily the best meal I'd eaten in years. Perhaps they weren't going to enslave us after all.

After eating, we four paired off to better fit into the Avavares' family-sized huts. Estevanico and Dorantes went to stay with their medicine man, while Núñez and I boarded with an ordinary family. The father and mother spoke with us, but their kids kept to themselves; they were too young to understand most Marianes phrases.

"So, are you the foreigners who healed the dying people of the east?" the father asked. "We've been told about how you saved lives."

My mind immediately went back to the dying Cavoques boy that Asturiano had saved on the island. But otherwise, I hadn't seen any miracles in the past six years. I doubted if Núñez had been much of a healer either.

"Yes, that's us," Alvar Núñez said with a smile. I looked at him, surprised by his burst of confidence. "I managed to save a man who'd been shot with an arrow. I cut the shaft right out of his chest." Pride adorned his face. In that moment, I realized how little I knew about Núñez's time alone. All I knew was the squat bear of a man from many years before. Except now, his muscles were lean and his wide frame was not full.

"There was also a dying boy saved on an eastern island," I added. "But the foreigner who saved him is long gone."

"I see," the father said. "So you are indeed these men." I shrugged and Núñez nodded.

The mother added her thoughts. "How did you ever do such things? You look as tired and hungry as every other man." She was right; Núñez's eyes in particular were swollen black circles.

Núñez peered at her inquisitively. "I don't quite know myself," he said. "But I bet there's nothing we can't set right."

What had he been thinking? Núñez's cockiness seemed more like credibility to the Avavares, and they soon wanted to test our supposed skill. Was this his way of having fun?

"I'm sorry," he said to me that night. "I got overexcited."

I snorted a mild laugh. "I never knew you to be so foolish, Núñez. Or so excitable. In fact, I don't think I've seen you excited by anything before."

The short Spaniard lifted his hands in puzzlement. "It must be the prickly pears. I haven't eaten much fruit in a while."

Though his confusion seemed benign, I suspected there was more behind Núñez's personal change. A passion expressed itself where once he showed none.

"You won't be joking when the Avavares start asking for your help," I said bluntly.

"I know," he said, now matching my tone. "I'm already worried."

It is worth noting that before our arrival, the medicine man was the Avavares' undeniable leader. While he may not have wielded the same civic power as their elders, he was their spiritual heart and hope. All this changed with Núñez's comment. A group of Avavares entered our family's hut in the afternoon, hoping the medicine man wouldn't notice.

"We would have gone to him," they said. "But we heard how skilled you are, and he hasn't been able to help. Will you come with us?"

"Of course we will," I said, slapping Núñez on the back. "My friend here is an expert." It was time for Alvar to substantiate his claims. He practically growled at me for the reminder.

We filed into a hut not too far off. The sight wasn't horrible; all we saw were a few sitting indís, normal enough, moaning from some sort of headache. The ailment may not have been severe, but how was anyone to fix it?

"Please heal them like you healed the others," the Avavares requested.

Núñez stood there blankly, as if he had not actually expected their request to feel so real so quickly. An awkwardness filled the room from the absence of action. Worry and fear plagued the minds around me. I remembered what the missionary Asturiano had told me—that God healed through him rather than he on his own. What could go wrong if I gave it a try?

"Don't worry, Alvar," I said. "You can stand right there."

I approached the closest indí, placing my hand on her forehead like some sort of medical miscreant. *God, if you're listening,* I thought to myself, *then it'd be really nice if this worked. I've seen people change their mood before, from kind-hearted to angry, and my failure today could cause that. I don't know how badly these people need this, but I know I do.* My mouth started rambling words I wasn't listening to, unintelligible thoughts from my heart. *I couldn't tell you why I'm here, but I feel like this act is necessary. Have your way; do what you will.*

I brushed my hand against the heads of the other indís before returning to those that had brought us. "They'll be fine in the morning," I said. "Let them sleep."

Walking back to the family's hut that day, I felt instantaneous regret. I had gotten more carried away than even Núñez. This would be a much harder hole to dig us out of.

The following morning arrived, and the Avavares flooded the family's hut.

"Thank you," they said to me. "Thank you; you are as skilled as we'd heard."

I sat there overwhelmed, hearing from the Avavares how I had healed them all.

I finally turned to Núñez. "Do you think their headaches must've passed? Maybe we arrived at the tail end of the sickness."

He frowned. "It's just as unlikely that they would have all ended at the same time. I don't know, Castillo... how'd you do it?"

"Really?" I asked. "You really think I made this happen?"

Núñez shrugged. "Seems about right."

"I didn't do anything," I said. I stopped for a moment. An image of the missionary Asturiano dead somewhere in the plains came into my head. "All I did was let Him work through me."

Núñez chuckled. "Well... thanks be to God. I guess."

I broke into a smile. "I guess so."

My soul ached at the adoption of such foreign rationale. But somehow, beside myself, I breathed a sigh of relief.

CHAPTER 18

The Burning Bush

———

ALVAR NÚÑEZ

October 1534

Whatever Castillo did, it sure awarded us a lot of meat. The Avavares brought handfuls of venison into the family's hut, and we gorged ourselves; they also gave some to Andrés Dorantes and Estevanico, though it did perplex their medicine man host to learn Castillo had performed his job better. Or God had, rather. I was yet be convinced one way or the other.

The problem with vast amounts of meat is that you get hungry again. When that time inevitably came for me, as well for my companions, we were informed of the Avavares' usual practice. "The village always migrates this time of year," the father of the house said. "There's a better crop out there now; but we'll come back here in due time."

I reasoned with Castillo and Dorantes whether to move along with our hospitable hosts or to use this shift as an opportunity to continue onward. My instincts told me to remain in safety. "It's nearly winter," I said. "And these have been the kindest people to us thus far. I think it'd be best to stay with them awhile longer." My companions all agreed, so we followed the Avavares across the barren plains.

The crop we now chased was the spring vetch, a bitter legume; we branched off with the Avavares men to gather these beans. Women were usually the gatherers, but the men opted to take these roles when the tribe traveled in unfamiliar territory. The Avavares men led us into the nearest stretch of woods, without paths or trails to guide our steps. I spent several days scouring the area in search of the crop. The vetches sat encased in noticeable purple flowers, but I came up short in my search. The hunger was starting to drive everyone to lethargy, even the toughest indís, and they were all ready to move on to another place. I, on the other hand, had this feeling that I might soon starve if I didn't find any beforehand.

"We're going to head to the new huts with them," Castillo said to me. It was nearing midday. "They want to regroup before we look elsewhere."

"You really think you'll find food back there?" I asked.

He shrugged. "We haven't found any this way."

"I'm too hungry," I said, grimacing. "I'm going to go further in; there must be some nearby." The forest was a wide, expansive series of spaced-out trees and tough soil. Beans had ample room to hide.

"Alright," Castillo said. "But don't fool yourself long enough to starve. The natives won't bury you if they can't find your body."

I nodded with all sincerity. "Come fetch me if you find anything," I said, then started walking away.

The surrounding shrubs showed no sign of the food I needed, so I took my strides even deeper into the wood; not a single flowering bulb readily invited me. My feet went over an endless stretch of upended stones and fallen dry branches which jutted from the dirt. Missteps were a risk over the rough terrain, but hunger drove me to walk even quicker. For perhaps an hour I stepped in perfect rhythm, ignoring each sharp pain and the many sores on my feet; the brisk air made me feel all the more naked.

Despite the cold air, the sun was merciless. The trees stood much shorter than any reliable height, and they failed to shade even me from consistent sunlight. I wished there was a way to spare myself from the sun's damaging rays, but my skin always soaked them in. Layers easily peeled off. Ever since my travels as a merchant, my skin had begun to tear apart like snakes' scales. Twice per year a layer shed off completely. Nagging pain always followed.

For hours I went on without rest, scurrying through a web of barriers in search of my food. Sharp thorns kept cutting at my sides as I pressed on; I never looked to the ground, determined not to miss what I was looking for. A long string of padded steps dulled my senses until I stepped on the sharp end of a broken reed.

I cursed. The reed made a deep gash in the bottom of my foot.

Sitting down, I stared at my injury a while, trying to examine what damage had really been done. Blood flowed from the deep incision, while dust already clung to the wound; the reed had entered my sole, but thankfully had not splintered. Regardless, it hurt enough to make me forget about my hunger.

If I wanted to spare myself from an infection, I would have to head back to the Avavares. So I rose and hobbled back in the direction from which I came.

Pretty soon, three facts made themselves clear: first, the sun never runs perfectly east to west in a day (I already was aware of this, but it had never frustrated me so much before). I tried to follow the sun's bright position many times, but it never led me to the river where the temporary village was being assembled. As a second fact, I realized that I had been gone long enough for my companions to have walked ten miles in any direction; this did not bode well.

The third fact I realized is when you are lost, you know it.

Skylight began to darken, and as much as it displeased me, I knew the tribe was too far off to reach in daylight. Above all, I needed to stay alive, which meant warmth and water were necessary by the nighttime. *Think, Alvar,* I said to myself. *You've survived lonely nights before.* Granted, those lonely nights typically had occurred with a Mediterranean villa or a native lodge nearby.

Cold air was overwhelming the fading sun. My poorly-padded bones ached for comfort. Wrapping myself into fetal position, I tried to regain heat before looking for a water source again. I greatly missed my thick indí coat. But however badly I wanted to remain huddled, my life depended on a successful search. I stood once more to face my trial.

For endless meters I frantically scoured. Then, faintly, I could smell it: a forest fire, right in the middle of the desert wood.

This is impossible, I said to myself. With any usual fire, the flames would have spread to other trees, shrubs, and dry plants; walls of heat could have easily entrapped me. Blazed forests had killed many a man in Spain. But to my amazement, in this strange forest there burned one lone tree. The lone tree kept burning, self-sustained.

Moses had apparently seen the Burning Bush, but had he ever been stuck naked in a wooded wasteland, struggling to find some beans? Here I was, the man without dignity, seeing a weirder version of this famed wonder.

I slept as close to the fire as I could.

The tree was still ablaze when I woke up. I marveled at the sight. For seemingly the first time, my survival had been contingent on a force outside myself. Was this also something I'd have to thank God for?

Regardless, I was determined to take the matter of survival back into my own hands. I had in my desperation traded discovering a water source to take advantage of the strange miracle; but now, I felt an overwhelming thirst. I embarked to find a stream and came across one lying far off. Its flow was too wrong to have been connected to the river I still sought (as a landmark for the tribe), which meant I needed to make a plan for how to get back to the others. I drank, washed my swollen foot, and went back to the tree, still remarkably caught in its flames. It was beginning to make sense to me: if God had gone out of his way to keep the fire going through the night, why would He stop once the sun came up? Nevertheless, I thought it best to make sure the fire never went out. So first, before I went anywhere else, I lit a branch as a torch.

Cauterization had never appealed to anyone before, and I was no different. But the deep gash had yet to heal or close over. I didn't want to worry about infection any longer, so clenching my teeth, I held the torch to my open wound. Despite the miserable sting, the precaution was necessary. Finally I could freely walk again.

After a moment's rest, I found myself in a tough position. Finding the village was my motivation, above all, but I also needed to make sure I had reliable flame. With deliberation, I decided to collect more dry wood to keep the fire burning. I then searched for two suitable branches to become torches, given that two were all my hands could carry, and that walking with them safely was a careful maneuver. *Time to get moving*, I muttered to myself. With lit torches in hand, I left the burning tree and pursued what I thought to be the proper direction to my companions. It had taken three days with company and one day alone to come upon this part of the desert woods; if I was lucky, it would take about as long to get out.

I rushed forward as much as possible, knowing that by evening, I needed to have found a place by the water where I could set myself for the night. My entire day was spent in anxiety. I found a stream (possibly the same one) at around sunset, looked for firewood, stocked it into a pile, and lit it with my left-hand torch. I considered there might be problems with just one source of fire. Snakes, namely, liked to creep up at night and strike a leg with venom. So, using the light from my first, I built three more around the area; in total they made a circle with a ten-foot radius. I tried my best to settle to sleep in the dim warmth and protection of that circle, my body immediately shivering from intense chills and my mind captivated by dreams of food. Frequently I rose throughout the night to tend to the four flames. I barely slept at all, mainly from the cold, and so my already weakened figure was left damaged for another day of frantic maneuvering.

First chance in the morning, I drank my fill from the stream. The rest of the day was to be spent exactly like the last, except with a greater emphasis on providing myself with warmth. I pulled two burning branches from each pile, then stamped out the four fires so they could not spread. I walked for hours, never stopping, never saying a word to myself, until I finally had an idea to make the night more survivable.

At another prime location by water, I set the fires like I had before, but this time dug a pit in the middle of the circle. It ran two meters long and about one meter deep, all dug with nothing but my hands. I didn't eat so much as a worm. At this point it was only late afternoon, so I got the idea to make myself a blanket from blades of tan wheat-grass. Long grasses like these grew all over the country. I picked as many pieces as I could find, then tied them all together as best I could. The blanket looked thick and very fibrous, though holey, and the process took me well into the night. Putting my creation around me, I finally sat in the pit and tried to drift to sleep.

My body was under too much stress to dream, so I instead let sleep hit me soundlessly, doing its best to repair the damages of hunger. Warmth could be felt, even in my rest, and I never once thought of waking.

But the warmth rapidly grew too hot.

My eyes opened, surrounded by night, and my body was lined in sweat. The brightness of the flames was spreading, all over me in fact, completely covering the blanket in a mass of fire. I yelled. I yelled again, unhinged. Flames were right in my eyes; I tried to toss off the burning bundle I made for myself. The blanket flew off and I scrambled out of the pit. I looked down, horrified. My beard was on fire. I crawled on all fours, rubbing my face against the dirt, until I finally could touch my cheeks without my fingers getting burned.

The flames had been snuffed, yes, but my hair had been scorched, leaving singed and flaking patches on my head, face, and neck. Burns were everywhere, lining the surface of my skin. Had I tempted God by attempting to harness his miracle? I sat outside the pit for the rest of the night, wondering when the winds might have changed to cause me such torture.

For three more days I ran through the woods with my two torches. I was a desperate, crazy naked man who had been burnt to a crisp, and I did not want to stop running, even if the sky became pitch black. Ravenous, I thought of nothing but getting to eat again.

On the third day I finally heard sounds from a powerful stream flowing ahead of me. I slipped past the final barrier of sparse trees, glad to see the familiar river. This was certainly the river where the village had been, I knew it in my protruding bones. The torches slipped out of my hands. I wasted no time in beating out their flames, like any victor might his enemy. I was no victor.

Fresh, flowing water invited me to drink my fill, so I sipped from the edge of the bank as would a roaming head of cattle on a hot summer day. Thirst sated, I thought again of hunger. I looked along the riverbank for as far as my eyes could see; well into the distance, I spotted the smoke of the Avavares. Thankfully, they were on my side of the shore. With only a half day's travel along the river, I could finally tell them I had not been lost for good.

Before sundown, I arrived at the group of huts. The indís quickly approached me as I walked on.

"Is that you?" they asked. "You look horrible. Come get some food."

Of course they knew I was hungry: I looked it. Perhaps I had lost fifty pounds, but from exactly when I could not say; pounds made little difference for someone that emaciated. My hosts gossiped about me as I ate. Covered in burns, hair missing in the oddest places, and skin peeled from nearly every crevice; with bulging sores on my back, and bloody cuts all over my feet, there had probably never been a man so worn down. Yet I had found my way back, and to me that was all that mattered.

A thought continued to haunt me, however: if I had accepted the Burning Bush as it was, and not manipulated it to my benefit, would my body have remained unscathed? With each downward glance at my patched figure, I became more certain my resoluteness was the cause.

CHAPTER 19

Holy Resuscitation

ANDRÉS DORANTES

Avavares Territory, 1535

The Medicine Man sat at the head of his hut like a king on a throne. His home, this pitched hut, had been my dwelling since the first day we encountered the Avavares. The home was larger than any, bar the hut where the elders convened. Why was his hut so large? Well, it was because he housed children, many of them, and he had two young wives who continued to give him many more. But his children were not the ones sitting at his feet today, as it might have usually gone. No... today it was none other than myself and Estevanico listening to the Medicine Man's tale. His story had no place with the likes of children.

"A man walked here many years ago for a time which lasted a full season. He came only to the Avavares, and we are still shaking from his presence." The Medicine Man stared intensely, caressing his chin. "His beard looked rough, brown, and curt. His head sat just below any of our kin, like a child in his height..." The Medicine Man extended his hand as a marker, referencing the supposed height to be near his chest. "His eyes could be seen at a distance; they were sneering, tawny eyes which seemed like beads from afar. These eyes were only one part of a face which looked like the sickly pale of a waning moon." The Medicine Man coughed, not necessarily from any sickness. "He would not stay away from our gatherings, and he first appeared at our ceremony in the winter; he sat in a place off away from the fire, right near some of the women. Most did not see him in this corner, but the women sitting close by could see him there... and they were trembling. He simply sat there, wearing a large hide like a woman might, though only to blend in enough to sit by them. His features, and all the windows to his heart, were unclear. There was the slightest grin that could be seen. So the woman built her courage, and she asked him where he lived. He just pointed... right at the ground in front of him. 'From beneath you,' he said to her. She was left frightened, even after he had left."

I raised my brow. "And what became of all this?"

"We just went on dancing, even when it was very dark," the Medicine Man said. "It was like any other celebration: we circle around the fire in a moving wheel, jumping and kicking our legs as we keep spinning. In that night's celebration, we got lost, just like we are supposed to. But when we lost ourselves in the dance, we did not notice the man join our circle." The Medicine Man dwelled on this recollection. "He danced around with us for an unknown amount of time; but finally I opened my eyes, looking ahead in this circle. There he was, with his clouded eyes staring directly at mine; he was dancing our dance in the clothes of a man, with the slightest grin on his face. So I watched him in shock for a while, and my shock made me useless against the things he might do. He knew this. He stole slowly out of the dance, and then took many steps to walk over to my hut. He grabbed the entire hut and did an unbelievable thing: he lifted it above his head."

The Medicine Man paused for a while. "It stayed there for a moment, and I watched it, until he at last threw it to the ground. Of course, our dance halted because the sound shook my people from their trance. We all looked to him, and he was still there, not afraid of anything we would do. When he left, it was unannounced and in an instant. It took me a long time to make sure that we were really all alone; we could not find him. The woman who had talked to him then told us about his answer to her question, and she started to cry. None of us were able to comfort her, or to sleep that night after seeing him. I named him The Bad Thing."

Estevanico extended his legs to stretch. "Did you see him again?" he asked.

"Yes. He came back whenever he liked," the Medicine Man said. "He happened to come when we wanted him least... in the night. The Bad Thing took whomever he liked from out of their huts, all while they were sleeping. They were dragged off, by the light of his unearthly torch, out into the fields. We would find them there in the morning, always mangled in the same way. We looked at their bodies and could only imagine the horror of their encounter with The Bad Thing. He could have slaughtered us all the same terrible way."

The Medicine Man went on to relate the method of their deaths. The description was too outrageous for me to accept as truth. Estevanico, struck by the outlandishness, felt the same way; we both held back our reactions until he finished his tale.

Our responses luckily did not offend the old man, but he felt the need to prove his story's truth. The Medicine Man told us to fetch Núñez and Castillo so that they might see his proof as well; we went to their hut, asked them to come, and then followed the Medicine Man where he intended. They had heard the same tale from their hosts nearly two weeks ago, and both had our same reaction.

The Medicine Man took us a mile outside the village, into the open plains. A burial ground seemed to be our destination, though it looked nothing like what I was used to seeing: several above-ground caskets littered the land in scattered positions, all woven together by the twigs of fallen trees. I had not taken the time to studiously observe local burials, as the thought never really occurred to me. It soon became obvious the Avavares kept these bodies preserved in one form or another; otherwise, the flesh would not still have been on the opened corpse. But why had his corpse not deteriorated more? The Medicine Man tore through the tangle of wood which covered the body of his long-lost kinsman, only to reveal a ghastly sight in its purest. The scene matched everything he had described: a large, swollen mark beneath the ribs, three long scars on the left arm, and a stomach so shrunken it could give a soldier nightmares. Black beads were left in place of what should have been the dead man's eyes, and a lethargic look had set in before he died.

With the evidence before me, I slowly accepted the Medicine Man's unspeakable terror to be true. The Bad Thing, years ago, had stolen this man from his hut, and by the light of his unearthly torch had taken him out into the open fields. With a knife made of rusted flint, he stabbed him deeply beneath the ribs; he followed this by reaching inside his stomach, widening the hole, and grabbing hold of his intestines. He unraveled them from inside the man, pulling his body's entire inner-workings out onto the dry ground. The Bad Thing cut a piece and burned it for the sake of his evil gain. Three slices on the left arm were made with the rusted knife, one in a place to bleed the man out... if he had not died already, there was by then no hope for him. This beast, simply for his own amusement, then sealed every wound with the power of Hell; only scars would be left over from his torture. The Bad Thing broke the then-dead man's arm and reset it improperly, leaving his body out to be found in the morning.

If the power of God was evidenced by Castillo's miracles and Núñez's return, then this disturbing corpse was my proof of Satan.

I saw plenty more graves in that field, some maligned in the same awful way. Disbelief was further eked out of me with every relic of the dreadful place. I felt no need to speak to my companions; we were all undoubtedly considering this mysterious beast to be a wandering demon.

"I am living in constant fear that The Bad Thing will come back to us." The Medicine Man sat in the middle of his tribe's burial field, reeling from the emotion of looking at these upturned graves. He rocked back and forth ever so slightly to coax away the terrible images from his head. "This place is meant to be a somber shrine to our heroes of war. But now, after the crimes against us those years ago, it is nothing but a reminder of the unpredictable plight which might again befall us. I've stopped the dances which beckoned him here; I've done everything to keep The Bad Thing away. But I don't know what he really is. I have no clue if he wants to come back."

He started to cry.

It's always unsettling to see a staunch patriarch at his lowest. When the Governor had been sick, he hid himself away; the Medicine Man, however, was unashamed of his situation. Seeing him this way gnawed at me, and I felt uncomfortable. The Medicine Man's despair was a revelation of his people's true state-of-mind. Yet as much as his emotion may have been accurate, it did not behoove the health of the many to let this man stay overwhelmed with worry.

Castillo put his hand on the crouched old native's back, and like a friend he knelt down beside him. "I can tell you something," Castillo said. "That beast, The Bad Thing, won't be coming back. He's a spawn from Hell... and if he knows anything, which he does, there's not a chance he's getting anywhere near this village again. As long as we're near here, or as long as you take God's power to heart, then the beast's nothing more than a distant memory." The Medicine Man looked toward Castillo; his face was filled with sorrow, but he seemed undoubtedly reassured. How could he not trust the healer who had upstaged him? "You've got nothing to worry about any longer," Castillo said. He rose from the old man's side, and walked back with us to the native village. We left the Medicine Man alone to remember all the friends he had lost. I was not so confident as to whether more losses would follow.

Months passed, and the Bad Thing had not scared us away. We thus continued on in the Avavares' good graces, further garnering the respect of our native hosts.

Thanks to Castillo's miracles (with his nominal assistant Núñez), our tribe wanted us to work among the others who stretched across the region. At first I thought this meant we'd be moving around, but this was not the case. Willingly, these people traveled a good distance to accept blessings: the Maliacones, Atayos, Cultalchulches, Comos, and Coayos all came to the Avavares village at one time or another simply to reap the benefits of his prayers. They didn't always come at once (some of them hated each other), but they came in great numbers and at constantly growing rates. For every person healed, Castillo received another reward, and it felt as if no request could go unfulfilled.

Nevertheless, the recent pressures weighed heavily. Castillo came under quite a deal of stress, as all of this spiritual work rested on his shoulders. He had yet to fail, but he feared that if he did, it would cause our enviable situation to crumble, losing us our earned favor. It was for this very reason I did not attempt to help. My head was shrouded in darkness; all I could think about was fearful grief for my brother and my home, and in no way could I have outwardly healed. Estevanico, only a half-hearted morisco, also had no chance. Alvar Núñez was a passive assistant only in that his strange features were a distraction for the people waiting their turn; he stood at the hut's entrance, making sure it was not too full by playing with the little children. He'd throw a stone for them to race after or make a stupid face when they grew tired of him throwing stones. This gate-keeping became his all-day job, while Estevanico and I worked among our hosts in practical tasks.

Castillo therefore held the full role of meeting the visitors' demands. He toiled through each day, speaking in strange tongues and praying between every visit; only when Castillo felt weak at the knees did Núñez rush in to perform his miracles. Núñez saw success perhaps once or twice, but he knew far less than Castillo about what powered his work. For Núñez the inspiration was purely tactical. For Castillo, I did not know where the inspiration came from. Was his faith genuine? Had he happened into this great power without full awareness?

April eventually arrived, and new tribes came in droves to clear their populace of lingering winter diseases. So great were their numbers that Núñez finally had to attempt full-time healing, or else half the indígenas would have died before Castillo visited them. Even still, most of his attempts failed, forcing Castillo to take on these problems anyway. Some cases were far more serious than others; but to every man or woman, their ailment is serious. They all wanted to see Castillo.

"I can't keep this up much longer," he said. We four were sitting together after a particularly rigorous day. "You know, these miracles... they're not me. I have no control over them one way or the other. I'm letting myself get carried away by all this, and it's making me lose my grip. I mean, I didn't even believe in a god, and now I'm preaching and praying to all these people, saying things to try to convert a shaman? What if I end up ruining it for the rest of you?"

"Nonsense," I said. "You're the only reason any of this is going on."

"But I'm a fraud," Castillo said, rather expressionless. "What if I'm just testing God's patience? I thought He was only doing these miracles to buy us time, but we haven't moved anywhere in months." Castillo's hollow face made a cavern seem like a field. "Maybe we're making Him wait too long."

Núñez butted in. "It doesn't do you any good to talk like that. There's food here, and water, and the people think they need us. He probably had some reason for us to stay here a while. When it makes sense to leave, we will."

Castillo didn't answer. It hurt his head to think. He needed rest.

The three of us laid him comfortably on his sleeping quilt, a gift given by the Comos tribe. "What are we going to do tomorrow?" Estevanico asked. "There's no way he'll wake up with enough strength."

Núñez nodded. "It seems we'll have to fill in for him."

Estevanico shrugged. "I'll be worthless at it."

Núñez ignored the doubt, his mind falling into reflection. "I've been too hesitant to trust that any of this is divine," he said. "I keep explaining away my survival and Castillo's miracles. I try to impose my own agenda on every gift presented to me. If I instead embrace the absurd, maybe things will work out better..." He looked to me for approval.

I paused, very hesitant to agree with him. I had been in a fog for months on end; I witnessed my brother burnt to a crisp, and yet Núñez was brought back from the flames. I had seen proof of hell's wrath on this country, and yet had been compelled to embrace it by lies of opportunity. Slowly, I was beginning to make sense of what my unfamiliar life had become, but still I longed for my ideal life on the long-lost family farm. My father's dying wish had ruined my life, and I did not have the faith to heal any soul but my own.

I might have voiced these concerns if not for Estevanico. I could not make myself vulnerable to my prisoner. Instead, I assented to Núñez. "I will see you both in the morning," I said. "Make sure to pray tonight for good luck."

When the Susola tribe arrived at dawn, the three of us rose to action. They had arrived later than the other tribes, by almost two weeks in fact; however, this delay was necessary to avoid the Comos, their embittered enemies. The Susolas were also in bad relations with the Atayos, who were still visiting, and the two tribes set up separate temporary villages on opposite sides of the Avavares territory. Fortunately, for the sake of benefiting from us, the rivals managed to avoid contact with each other.

The Susola chief spoke with Núñez. "Quickly! We have waited long to see you, and our sick have grown sicker. You must get to them quickly."

"Take me to the worst of them," Núñez said.

The Susolas brought us toward the sickest man in the tribe. He was a well-liked young archer who had been in search of a good wife when he suddenly fell ill from a disease no one had much experience curing. There were bumps and such all about his body, they told us. I had seen similar ailments eat away the lives of several natives thus far.

When we approached the hut where he was being kept, the Susola women told us the hut did not belong to him, as his own had been taken apart and given to others who needed the materials. People were outside the hut and many were weeping. It was the fixture of a memorial.

I whispered to Núñez. "He must be dead."

"I think you're right," he said. Regardless, we decided to enter the hut.

I immediately smelled fresh death. The corpse below me was a young man dead no more than a day, swollen red with hives and open sores. The people knew his current condition, but they hadn't buried him.

"We're too late," I said.

"I won't be the one to determine that," Núñez said.

Núñez kneeled beside the body, watching for any sign of movement. I don't know why he wasted his time. The indí's eyes had rolled to the back of his head, and his lips had turned black; his heart skipped every beat. A woman near Estevanico cried loudly, and he did all he could to reassure her. His reassurances were little more than empty promises. None of us had ever raised a man from the dead.

Núñez lifted off the deerskin blanket which covered the man's torso, throwing it aside. He breathed slowly on the corpse, as if it were a necessity; by the look on his face, I almost believed it was. The indígenas watched him, full of angst, as he whispered indiscernibly over the lifeless form. Núñez paused, a perplexed expression taking over his strange features. He bowed his head and began to weep. At first, his tears came lightly, though soon grew to uncontrollable sobs; he leaned over the fallen man, begging for a work that wasn't his.

CHAPTER 20

Sedentary

———

ESTEVANICO

The Avavares Territory, Spring 1535

Alvar Núñez reclined in the hut near to where Castillo was sitting. For Núñez, the act had been a sacred one, a happening which traumatized him. He observed the wood wall linings and the quilt on the floor with humbled, trepidatious glances. I stood at the entryway by Andrés Dorantes, watching our companion regain his bearings.

"All I remember is my deep sorrow for the man," Núñez said. "It brought me to my knees." He closed his eyes and breathed in.

Castillo stirred him from his rest. "So you saved the indí?" he asked.

"That's what they told me," Núñez said.

"Oh, now we're really in for it," Castillo said. He turned away from the short, freakish Spaniard.

Andrés Dorantes moved to sit by the others. We were in the home of Núñez and Castillo's familial hosts, not the Medicine Man's lodge, but Andrés made himself comfortable nonetheless. "What are you complaining about, Castillo?" he asked. "You don't like having someone to share the load?"

Castillo shook his head. "No, that would've been fine. But what Núñez just did raises their expectations tremendously."

Núñez smiled. His visible teeth were disproportionately pleasant compared to his disfigured face. "Castillo, you've held trust this far. I'm a bit surprised by how scared you are all of a sudden."

"I'm not scared," Castillo said. "I'm exhausted... and unhappy with the prospect of doing this for much longer."

I thought to myself from my place in the entryway. Castillo's complaints were ironic considering the amount of praise he had received; I suppose it does not matter what the work's rewards are when an inner desire has not been filled.

"It's certainly better than being a slave," Núñez said. He was correct. "Think about what else we could be doing right now."

"We could be moving forward, is what. Nueva España lies ahead, and then our passage back to Iberia itself." Castillo sighed. "Soon enough, we'll be stuck in these roles; the indígenas won't want us to leave. I didn't come to La Florida just to become a doctor like my parents back home. I escaped that kind of life. I'm looking for adventure, not whatever this is."

At this more audible display, the host family rose to leave from where they were quietly talking. They opted to give us a moment alone in their own home.

Núñez seemed not to notice their exit. "So you're unexcited," he said, his arms folded prescriptively. "You aren't stimulated by a life of healing."

Castillo chuckled. "I'm not so weak that I need everything to excite me; but thank you for thinking that. What I'm actually trying to say is these past months have upended me. I embrace all the things I used to turn away. I need space to gather myself, to decide what I really believe about all of this. Otherwise, I'll end up in a place I don't even recognize."

"Unfamiliarity is what adventure's all about," Núñez said. "Sorry, my young friend, but I think they mis-sold you on it."

Castillo blushed; he had an aversion to being reduced to naïveté. "What's your reason for wanting to stay?" he asked. "Do you prefer fake doctor work to the soldiering you're meant for?"

Núñez frowned; an encompassing tension prevailed. Andrés Dorantes began to look uneasy with the situation. "I'll go take care of the indís tomorrow," he said. "One day off will hopefully be enough to get you out of your sour mood, Castillo. And for you, Núñez, to help you reexamine your attachments." Andrés stood up from beside his frustrated countrymen. "I'll see you in the morning; you two can manage whatever menial tasks they were going to give me." Andrés walked past me, out the entryway, and toward the Medicine Man's house.

Núñez turned right back to Castillo. "I, too, have been upended by all this. But I'm figuring out where I stand as we move along strategically: I'm not planning our next departure with my mental state as the prime consideration." The short Spaniard stared at his slender companion, and the latter remained silent. "That being said, I'm not unreasonably opposed to leaving here. As long as we can handle what the Avavares demand, I think it's in our best interest to stay through the season and slowly shift away from our new roles. But, if we physically cannot continue this healing, then I will agree to moving on. What do you say to that?"

Castillo nodded. "Yes, whichever of those two comes first, then we should leave." He closed his eyes and leaned his head against the wall. "Let's see how Andrés manages tomorrow. We both know how uncertain this whole phenomenon is."

In hearing Andrés' name mentioned alongside the act of healing, a chill shot through my spine. This was the man who had benefited from my tragedies, who used his free will to impose everything but the power of healing on my life. I would rest terribly knowing God had bestowed the likes of him to perform the works of much, much better men. Beyond that, I needed to know that my hands and my prayers, passed on by my forefathers and nearly forgotten, were as suited to the miraculous as the hands and prayers of these two doting Spaniards. Could I let this life pass without proving my deepest beliefs to be just as valid?

"I'll help him tomorrow," I said. "It'll give you a better estimate of when to leave."

My declaration somewhat surprised Castillo and Núñez, but they eventually nodded.

I left the two doting Spaniards to their slumber.

CHAPTER 21

Wandering

ALONSO DEL CASTILLO

1535

I could not handle another day. The same entrapping hold of the University had found me in the wilderness. Did it make any sense to cross the Atlantic, only to become what my father and mother already were in Salamanca? I strongly believed not, and I felt the urge to move along.

At first, Andrés Dorantes and Estevanico kept the native visitors at bay. Estevanico managed to heal several ailments which were presented to him, while Andrés served him by occupying the children and those in waiting. "You're right," Andrés eventually said to me. "We need to leave. I can't keep crowd managing while Estevanico is in there saying little prayers." His dissatisfaction was a blessing to my ears. I took Andrés over to where Núñez was harvesting prematurely-ripened prickly pears. The scarred Spaniard had a content, serene smile as he picked the fruit; regardless, we pressured him to leave.

"Think about what you can do on a return voyage," I said. "The officials in Nueva España will probably be impressed, and they'll give you another fleet's worth of men and supplies. We need to keep moving, though, to get there."

Núñez looked at me hesitantly. "I don't know..." he said. "What would another expedition gain me when I'm already out here?"

I scratched my head. "Well, at least you should return to tell everyone what we've done. The world would be interested to know our story."

Hearing my logic, as well as Andrés' continued complaints about the nature of his work, Núñez acquiesced into leaving.

Núñez's one condition was that we tell our hosts about the departure. "They've been the kindest locals to us thus far," he said. "It feels too abrupt to exit unannounced." I was initially fine with this condition, but Estevanico soon informed us of a growing demand for our return to healing. With any announcement, the Avavares and the visiting tribes would protest our decision vehemently, he said. Secrecy was required. "Can I at least tell the family who's housing us?" Núñez asked. Estevanico shrugged impartially, but Andrés and I were opposed. Yes, the Avavares had been a good-natured people to live with; but after becoming their constant miracle worker—and hardly knowing how or why—I felt no pain in parting ways. With my sanity at stake, I needed to think about my own needs.

The four of us ventured off into the night.

Weeks passed in aimless wandering. Our efforts pivoted to searching for reliable guides. Any hope of reaching Nueva España on our own accord had been lost.

Nine women eventually became our guides. The inter-tribal war of 1534, the conflict which had allowed us to escape our earlier enslavement, had ruined the balance of their lives. These nine women from various fighting tribes all opted to wander the desert rather than become unnecessary collateral in their husbands' war. They found us, knew of our doctoring, and respected this reputation enough to offer their assistance. "You can only trust a woman in these parts," they had said. "The men might use you as leverage in the war. And besides, we know how to gather food they can't even identify." In return for their help, the nine guides demanded our compliance with their practices, which included waking, laboring, traveling, and resting at set times.

The Susola woman was the strongest; she also originated from the nearest tribe, which meant she knew our surroundings better than anyone. I asked her where we were heading. "There's a place where the river is easiest to cross," she said. "If you're looking to meet back with your people, then south from there is our best direction." The river she referred to had been a fixture of my horizon for years. It seemed vast in places, though spanned less than a few feet elsewhere. We had probably crossed it before at one of its more manageable stretches; this, however, was the first time we were actively deciding to leave it behind. No longer would it mark my horizon.

We followed the women like a flock of birds over the thinnest nearby point on the river. With a trek southward as our only hurdle, my mind began to picture what Nueva España might be like. None of us had ever been briefed on the nature of life there for Spaniards; I thus had many curious questions I wanted to see the answers to. I wondered especially about warm beds.

Our journey south weaved us on a thread from tribe to tribe throughout the summer. I swiftly began to doubt the morality of these Southerners. They were hospitable, to be certain, but they had a penchant for thievery; in fact, theft was considered acceptable. They even stole meat out of pots with their bare hands. Assuming this trait was regionally shared, I grew ever more possessive of my few acquired belongings.

Our encounters with new tribes mostly went as follows:

We'd enter a village, tired and hungry, and the hosts would usually provide these essentials, taking time to socialize with our guides. "What made you follow these men?" the hosts would ask. "They're following us," the guides would say. "And you obviously haven't heard the tales about them. They've done very strange things wherever they go, always from the east and never from the west. They are children of the sun." The hosts would become intrigued. "Children of the sun? What have these foreigners done?" Now, this is where the conversations varied. At first, it was only our guides who were there to mention, in great detail, the healing power which had overtaken us; it was all true, what the women said in this regard. But as we reached a new tribe, several of its members would decide to follow us, leaving their homes indefinitely. So when they, now a part of our ever-growing following, were asked what we had done, each gave his or her own twist on the many talents of the sun's children. "Erupting water from the ground" might be the subject of one such tall tale. "Leveling a forest of its trees" would be another.

But even as the mythos of the sun children grew, so did my unfamiliarity with this entourage. Our nine guides were content with their meager belongings, but whenever a new set of hosts fell asleep, other members of our gathering would take the opportunity to ransack the village. Cornmeal, tools, bows, arrows, hides, paints, nuts, fruits, and every imaginable item would be among us the following morning. It was a complete robbery, and it happened with every change of scenery.

My responsibility in the matter unsettled me. I spoke to Núñez. "I'm worried that this cultural custom will get us into trouble. What if we reach a village who does not share the tradition? It might derail our passage to Nueva España."

"Hmm..." Núñez gazed the short distance from his eyes to the ground. "This thieving habit might be within our control. Seeing how much I've changed because of the indís, it seems unlikely they are unaffected by our presence. What if they're stealing to try to impress us? A lot of the stolen goods have indeed been offered to us, as you're well aware."

I scratched my disheveled beard. Back in Spain, I had never been able to grow a beard. "That could be true," I said. "But how do we chastise these people when they almost all think this is fine?"

Núñez proposed a strategy. "There's no need to chastise. An ultimatum can be established: we make it clear they can only continue with us if they don't steal."

I nodded. "Good thinking."

I suggested the plan to the Susola guide. She insisted I allow her to be the one to communicate our thoughts to the loyal entourage. Fearing the task for myself, I happily agreed.

The Susola woman addressed her fellow indígenas; our mass following now consisted of a couple hundred. Most took the ultimatum well, with several indís shouting a question or two about our reasoning. The only native follower who did not agree to the proposal was a Maliacone woman. Our Susola guide talked the matter over with her for a short time, and eventually the Maliacone accepted our terms; nevertheless, she still wished to impart some of her reservations.

The Susola guide translated the Maliacone's words. "She feels you are considering your own motivations above all else," the Susola woman said. "So many have left their homes to follow you because of the wonders you are supposed to perform. But you are traveling quickly and performing none of these. People are disappointed; some are only still following you out of fear for what you will do to the disloyal. And now, she says, you are asking everyone to change their ways for you. She urges you to balance your expectations of yourself with what you expect of your followers."

I paused to think about the Maliacone woman's complaints. Were people truly afraid of us? "Tell her I see the merits of her complaints," I said to the Susola guide. "Those only following us out of fear should head back home; we won't do anything to them."

With that, our thieving problem was settled.

Eventually we reached a village of hogans built near the hillside. Mountains rose where they previously lay flat, rivers flowed for graciously long distances, and the dry tang of desert finally left its finest mark. Mesquite beans replaced prickly pears as the foremost fruit. They proved even harder to prepare.

As it happens, the people of this village anticipated our arrival and hid all their belongings, transplanting them elsewhere; we entered an empty world. A sole remaining object was the hallowed casing of a gourd. I asked one of the villagers about it. "The gourds float down from the beautiful rivers of the north," he said. "But only when the Heavens flood do they sail this far." The gourd had a hard orange exterior, with bands around the opening throat where an incision had been made. I assumed the tribe must have filled the gourd with something before sealing the hole. I reached out to pick it up. "No!" the villager said. "Don't touch it."

"Oh, sorry," I said, backing off. I wondered, however. "Why not?"

"These gourds have the power to heal, as much as I've heard you do. They're sacred, symbolic of the Heavens." He lowered his voice. "It should only be touched in ceremony."

I nodded. "Of course." I stared longer at the gourd, thinking about my so-called capabilities to heal. I had found God, I felt, in a land where I had come to find myself. Medicine had been my parents' tool in Spanish society, and newfound faith was my desert tool. But I had trouble picturing this version of myself in Spanish society. With Nueva España drawing ever nearer, would I fall back into faithlessness? Was my understanding of God even real?

An opportunity arose to once again put my faith to the test. The most respected men from our hosts spoke to our entourage guides, and the Susola woman relayed it to me, Núñez, Dorantes, and Estevanico in a language we understood. "They'd be honored to include you in a ceremony," she said. Her lean features relaxed as she sat down from our long trek. "They want you to bless the food, too."

"Seriously?" Dorantes asked. "Like praying over a meal?"

She shrugged. "They want your blessings; that's all they said."

Evening arrived, and we four children of the sun were each handed a sacred gourd.

The hosts spoke more with our guides. "No one's to eat a single thing until you each bless it," the Susola woman relayed. "I imagine you'll be very busy tonight."

"Bless the food individually?" I asked. She nodded. "You must be joking," I said. Apart from our entourage, the village hosts numbered slightly under five hundred tribes-people. Was blessing each meal even possible?

"I think we can do this," Dorantes said. "They've been cooking their meat well; our prayers won't have to be too convincing."

Núñez shook his head. "No, this isn't something to fake. We need to respect these miracles." The otherwise hard-boiled Spaniard had lately come across as sincere and reflective. His mind still reeled from what had been performed through him. My mind reeled from what still needed to be done.

I remembered, however, the Maliacone's assessment of our entourage, and their genuine desire for good works. "I agree with you, Núñez," I said. "We have reputations to uphold."

The village hosts asked us to sit in the center of their village, holding our gourds, while the people proceeded one by one to bring their food. Each person expected the prayer to last at least a few decent moments, and many also hoped for their health and household items to be blessed. I sat near an unlit fire pit with a straight back. Red dirt covered my bare bottom in paint-like fashion. Gourd in my left hand, and the power to dispel the native concerns in my right, I prepared to face the multitudes.

The eighth cooked quail of the night made its way into my reach.

"I bless this in the name of the Father, the Son, and the Holy Breath, that God might preserve her health and strength with this good meat," I mumbled in my native Castilian. "May no harm come of its consumption, and no ill come upon this woman Your child who eats it."

The woman, looking sixty and in suitable health for her age (for she was all visible in front of me), did not move. She stood in wait for further blessing. Estevanico sighed, then crouched over her ration of quail, breathing on it heavily. "My breath will make it good," he said in the tongue of an eastern tribe. "Go and eat it without fear." She finally left, satisfied by this additional display. Everyone in line now wanted the same holy breaths on their food, all because the woman had acquired them on hers.

Alvar Núñez was the most vigorous holy man. He developed a habit, though, of spitting when the dirt looked dry, turning back every once in a while to clear the phlegm from his throat.

At last, the line seemed to be thinning out; a man who had started way in the back was now right in front of me with his belongings. He set out a cactus, the stomach filet of a deer, and the wing of a dead bird. But next to all these he dropped a thin bracelet of copper quality. On the front someone had etched in a simple face, much like a small mural. The importance of this little trinket wasn't its design, however, but its material. I hadn't seen real copper in use for seven years.

"Where did you get that?" I immediately asked the man. He was unresponsive, confused. I tried again in a different tongue.

He looked at the bracelet. "This? I've had this bracelet with the face for years."

"Where did it come from?"

"I got this from the southwest," he said. "But these people are a many, many days' walk from where it was first made."

I brightened. "Do they craft other metal designs like this?"

He nodded. "Yes, they make lots of things that way. The metal is everywhere in the southwest, and they use it in every way. It is as valuable to them as the black leaves are to us."

The black leaves were simply thin mica slabs, which all the regional natives used as a currency in addition to their bartering items. Going by the man's words, the people to the southwest used copper, and possibly other metals, in the same way. It struck me as a very major development. My companions continued to pray, oblivious to the copper trinket.

"Would you be willing to give me this bracelet," I asked the man, "so long as I repay you with something else valuable in the coming days?"

He stood witless. "Well, yes, I think. If you could get me a full deer, I will give the bracelet to you."

Considering the rewards I usually received for blessings, I did not consider his request impossible. Someone in the entourage would surely hunt a deer in the coming days. "Absolutely," I said. "Thank you for your willingness."

He gave a nod. "My home is back there." He pointed to a hogan on the hillside. "Bring me a deer, and I'll give you the bracelet."

I smiled and commenced with the man's blessing. "May God bless your meat, and the plants of the earth, that you might gain substance from them, and consume them without issue. Bless the food to be a gift to him who eats it. I pray that, through Christ, all harmful things in this land are undone, and that this man won't see the forces of evil come upon him in the following years, or for all his days. Amen." I lightly elbowed Estevanico, who leaned over the venison, the cactus, and the boiled bird's wing. He blew generously the hot air which these natives found more calming than a flowing river. "Estevanico," I said. "Gather the other two when they finish. I found our first clear sign toward home."

CHAPTER 22

Rabbit Hunt

ANDRÉS DORANTES

En Route to the Copper Tribe, October 1535

The desert was uninviting, but it had created exceptionally resourceful residents. When all else seemed fruitless, our enlarged entourage took to hunting the jackrabbits of the plains. I was not about to stand by and watch them do it alone.

My foot-long club crashed hard against the dirt, sending red grains of sand into the air. I had barely missed the rabbit coming from its burrow.

I sighed, frustrated. "How am I supposed to catch a runt that runs faster than its own heartbeat?"

Estevanico chuckled. "I have no clue." He was sitting in the dirt, watching me hunt. "Are you giving up the chase, Andrés?"

"Well, it doesn't seem like you're planning to fill in for me," I said. "I'm going to kill it. Just wait right there and you'll see."

I continued the hunt. Though my life had been destroyed by La Florida and the wilderness to its west, I was managing to notice the beauty in my situation. There was a rhythm to our travels and my place in them, a rhythm which I had grown accustomed to. Discovering a tangible sign of home had resurfaced my long-held dreams to an extent, but I remained satisfied with each day's events. A rabbit hunt was one such event which pleased me.

Indígenas sprinted all around me with their bats in hand, completely crouching over the rabbit-holes. Hares jumped right into their grasp.

"Better keep up," Estevanico said to me. "You'll be wasting the strength in your legs if you come up empty." My father's slave glared at me smugly. I thought about when he had grinned right before Diego's death; he had found the chief's threats to my brother amusing. Had he been similarly amused by his death?

"Even if I come up empty, you still won't get any," I said. "Sitting there slacking won't earn you a rabbit."

"I never asked for one," Estevanico said. "I've chosen to miss this meal, and I'm rather enjoying taking a load off my back for a change." He sniffed in the fresh air. "Grunt work has grown tiresome, actually; I thought you might finally want to give it a try."

The club slowly slipped from my fingers as I turned to get a better look at my slave. He sat there cross-legged. Not a tame feature graced his face.

"You should think more carefully about what you say." I gave him a cold glance. "Remember where we're heading; remember who you are, Moor."

He stared at me rather blankly. "Andrés, I didn't mean any disrespect."

"Of course you didn't. But I get to decide what you meant, and I decide what you can say and do." I grabbed my club off the ground and turned back toward the desert plain. "Don't let this open air fool you, Estevanico."

"Yes, sir." He hung his head.

For Estevanico to ignore his place was one step too far; I had found some stability in this wilderness, but to lose my only relationship of dominance would overturn that development. A slave disobeying his master was too dissimilar from the life I intended. I needed to assert myself to ward off such humiliation.

When I found the perfect burrow, I crouched over it like the natives had and held my club in place. Soon, the hare darted from his home, but I stood right above. With one swift hit, the jackrabbit's back was snapped by the club; his front legs twitched until his spine stopped prompting movement. I lifted his carcass off the ground, walking out to hunt for more.

CHAPTER 23

Hearts in the Desert

ALVAR NÚÑEZ

Sonora, November 1535

Fleeting grasses grew far into the distance; I peered off and imagined their brush against my legs, though I never quite steered closer to them. Behind me, flattened mesas packed from russet boulders marked the deserts in scattered places. Ahead the hills were younger. Their summits pointed more intensely than any smooth mound of the north, and the sand had been brightened by a stronger sun. Cacti taller than the shortest giant, bitter to the tongue, grew from every plot of fruitless soil gracing the country. The heat of the day braised me on through the middle of autumn; but at night, the plains became an unforgiving tundra. Salamanders, spiders, worms, and burrowed moles had become a day's meal.

At last, my company of hundreds came into an inhabited region. Scouts approached us; they wanted to know why this massive crowd was visiting. Castillo had a more pressing question.

"Where was this made?" he asked.

The native, startled, examined Castillo's bracelet. "By the South Sea," he said, "where the rich rip metal from the ground to grow their wealth, but not to live. This place is beyond the mountains and rivers, where the world holds foreigners and the sun sets slowly."

When we answered the scouts' questions with tales of our exploits, they welcomed us openly to where their people resided. These Sonorans wore necklace beads and bison hides; they also smeared antimony metal on their faces like paint, with lines under their eyes and cheeks. They even gave little bags of silver to their guests. This must have been what the scout meant by using metal to live. Their silver deposits clearly held more than mere monetary value. How they ascertained to cast this metal with such limited means was beyond me.

Using our southernmost troupe members as interpreters, we asked the Sonorans for guidance to the South Sea. They refused, saying their neighbors in that direction were their bitter enemies. We suggested they could simply tell us the route, but they did not want our presence to grant their enemies an unforeseen advantage. I strategized with Castillo and Dorantes about how to convince them otherwise.

"We could just head south ourselves," Castillo said. "I mean, they did call it the South Sea."

"No," I said. "Especially not with old rivalries at stake. Our followers barely know this region as it is; we could very well become prisoners again with one misstep."

"I agree." Andrés Dorantes kneeled above the campfire, prodding it with dry sticks as the smoke began to rise. His hair looked nearly blond from exposure to the sun. "I think we should act mad. The Sonorans will be motivated to help if they believe we're angry."

Castillo hummed in thought. "Hmm... I could see that working if we played it up. But then again, it's a mean idea." He blew some slow air onto the budding flames.

I hesitated inside. The Sonorans had so far treated us with hospitality; I knew Dorantes was right, that they would never risk our potential befriending of their enemies unless we gave them no other choice. But if they believed the circulating rumors about our anger, then a simple threat would be an act of cruelty. "I don't know," I said. "I appreciate the importance of appearances, but it feels a little unnecessary."

Dorantes smiled, somewhat surprised. "Where's the soldier in you, Núñez? It's not like we need to threaten them with death. Let's just act guarded and upset by their refusal, then we can see what happens."

Castillo cleared his throat. "If you're convinced this will move us along, Andrés, I'll accept it."

I slowly nodded. "Okay."

That night, to display his supposed frustrations, Dorantes rejected the home they offered him and opted instead to sleep in the desert a half mile away. The Sonorans were left to figure out why he'd do such a thing.

Several more stunts of this nature were enacted. Our interpreter approached us about the issue. "The villagers are scared for themselves," he said. "No one here desires your anger, and they are begging you sun children to please forget your frustrations." Some Sonorans stood behind him, pointlessly pleading in their native tongue.

Dorantes shook his head. "We can't forget it."

Our interpreter looked confused. "Why?"

"Because," Dorantes said, lifting himself off the dirt, "they already know what we need from them, and they haven't made good on any of it." He wiped a coating of dust off his skin. "It's a matter of who they fear more: their enemies to the south, or the men from the rising sun. So far, it's clear who's been more intimidating."

"I see," the interpreter said. He looked displeased. "I'll tell them."

The Sonorans decided not to budge. They truly did fear their enemies more than the rumors about us.

I accordingly assumed we'd have to make a new plan for traveling ahead; however, over the successive days, the Sonorans suffered an unfortunate outbreak which had been ever so slightly building. The men, the women, and their many children lay inside the village homes, stricken by a sickness of incurable sores. I hadn't witnessed such sudden tragedy in months. Eight graves were dug in the time it took a hunter to catch his prey. The Sonorans had never come close to this level of mortality, and I doubt they considered us guilt-free. Our heightened anger looked to be the only culpable force. To them, it seemed the rumors about our wrath were proving true.

Dorantes drank sparingly from a clay jar of water in my hut. "I may sound insensitive," he said, "but I hope this illness changes their minds."

"Perhaps," I said with flaking lips. "But I wish their opinion wasn't based on this; they're so wary of us that they won't even risk me or Castillo trying to heal them. They might be dying needlessly right now."

Dorantes shrugged. "I thought it was never truly our choice whether to heal."

Another sorrowful three days passed in the village before our hosts had suffered enough.

The Sonoran chief, wearing nothing splendid, used our interpreter to explain what he intended. "My people's strength has been beaten into complacency," he said. "You win. You get what you want." Dorantes may have been smiling, but for me his words were hard to hear. I thought about the Charrucans who had given me a merchant's role for many years; if the same fate befell them, my grief would have been palpable.

The chief proposed our solution: two women would take leave in the direction of their enemies. One, their captive of a year-old battle, would serve as a goodwill token; the other, the Susola woman of our initial nine guides, could scout the territory before we considered following.

Days went by without an idea as to the women's progress; this gave some time for the village to recover. I watched impatiently through it all, with even the most desperately sick natives not wanting a blessing by our hands. Instead, the families were left to wallow at their loved ones' deaths. The camp had a dark cloud over it for many painful days. But as one family member died, the tears soon stopped falling down the cheeks of the living. These people of the desert had fortitude.

The last indígena to die was a young girl of perhaps fifteen or sixteen. She shivered through fever, moaned in pain, and coughed continually before finally succumbing to death's pull. A young boy, perhaps nine or ten, watched this girl through it all, bringing her water in a little clay jar whenever she looked to need it. The poor boy didn't have a clue how to save her; he wanted his sister to live as long as she could, but nothing slowed her impending passage.

This particular young boy was standing near me after her death. He looked over at me regretfully, like I could have done something to help. His lip, slowly, started to quiver, and tears welled beneath his eyes. The boy began to cry, but not like a child. He cried as someone who had seen far too much. Within minutes, he contained his crying and went about his life.

Our Susola guide returned and claimed the enemy tribe to be a safe host. She said the Sonorans had been granted clemency to take us there, but not to remain. We hastened our journey over.

A happy local informed us of the best routes to the South Sea. "We often take this one trail to kill the bovines in our neighbor's territory," he said. "They dislike us, but I'd say it's the safest way south for you."

"How long will it take to get there?" our interpreter asked.

"About twenty days," the happy local said. "There's a river flowing there, but it's hard to find food while en route."

"What food's available?" our interpreter again asked.

"Nothing except chacan." I could have mistakenly heard the name, but chacan was my best guess. The happy local brought us some of his chacan for reference. "You have to grind it first," he said. I put it in my mouth. The food was hard as a rock, and I cracked my teeth against it before inevitably spitting it on the ground. Chacan was frankly inedible.

"That's the only food on the way up?" I asked through our interpreter.

"Yes," the happy local said.

I frowned. "Is there a different route?"

He nodded. "Yes, the corn trail."

"We'll take that one," I said.

Castillo, Dorantes, Estevanico, and I soon departed on the corn trail with our native following in tow. Some number of them were not enthusiastic about heading this far into unfamiliar territory, so they went their separate ways.

Deep thirst overtook us on the corn trail. Not until our company came across a wide river did we find water. We drank heartily, then attempted to cross. Mothers and their children rode on our few canoes and the stronger men and women swam themselves to the other shore. I dragged myself out of the river, lying face-down against the sand. Each breath brought in another dose of choking dust; the same dirt stuck to my wet skin, blending together with my burnt color.

Mountains dotted the landscape on this side of the river. They were large mountains which outdid the heights of the Pyrenees in Navarre. Their stature inspired me; nevertheless, my current steps were taken on the low ground, between the peaks. My aching feet cracked over the same rocks as always.

Our struggles aside, we reached the corn trail's end in a relatively short period of time.

The people there spoke a language called Primahaitu. My mind had until that point operated in two linguistic spheres; on one end, I knew my native Castilian, as well as much of French, Català, Fiorentino, and Emiliano-Romagnolo. When I arrived in La Florida, and was forced to acclimate to different tongues, another sphere opened for me: Charrucan, Deaguanes, Han, and many other languages filled my head. In both these spheres, at least a distant relation of words and phrases could be found between varieties to make learning easier. For instance, the European languages I knew all hailed from the Latin of olden Rome, and therefore shared common traits at unexpected moments. There lived a people in Iberia, however, that did not glean even the most remote influence from Romans. These were the Basques. The Basque hills-people spoke their language, Euskadi, in total isolation for two thousand years, going opposite the trends of every other language in the southern Europe. While I've learned certain languages in a mere matter of weeks, I as an Iberian have never been able to grasp even a simple Euskadi phrase. It's so damn hard to speak like a Basque.

Primahaitu proved to be the Euskadi of this desert. All of our native followers had as much trouble as I did understanding it. An interpreter had to be found from among the Primahaitu.

Despite the language barrier, it became clear the Primahaitu were the most civil people I'd met since my arrival in La Florida. Their hillside houses were permanently situated, the women wore clothes and even moccasins, and their food grew well in every season; they had beans in the fall and summer, maize in the spring, and squash in the winter. There were no "prickly pear" field migrations or desperate seasonal hunts. No necessity was too far off. These were natives free from a life in poverty in every conventional sense. Turquoise, coral beads, and five emerald arrowheads were set before us as their guests. I looked out into their village and breathed in a deep, relaxed air. I could have been satisfied there for the rest of my life.

I began to pray small prayers over the villagers as they walked up to me, and in return, they would all place a bundle at my feet. By the end of the day, I counted six or seven hundred raw deer hearts in total from among these offerings.

Castillo scratched his peeling chin. "I just don't know how we're going to eat all this," he said.

I smiled. "That's a good problem to have."

I distributed one deer heart each to our native followers, but we still had enough left over to fill our Spanish stomachs for several meals.

This plentiful food was greatly appreciated in winter. Rains came in heavily, which inevitably served a nice change of pace from the desert heat. The weather might have struck a different man idle, but I chose to roam about with the most active men; I opted to join a lone hunter as he strode to catch a frenzied deer in its dash for cover.

Despite dull arrowheads and a short, tightly-wound bowstring, this hunter created an added advantage. By rubbing a certain tree's dark orange bulbs against the deadly edge, the man poisoned his shots against all prey and human enemies. He needed to prepare his arrows as such before he felt comfortable hunting. His calloused hands rummaged through the branches for this elusive orange berry, but by the hour's end had found nothing; the berry didn't grow well in winter. It was no matter. A resourceful man with some age to match, the indígena tore the weak bark off the tree which would eventually sprout these berries. Its tan, milky sap dripped downward; like a spider spinning a web, he rubbed his arrowheads in the poisonous flow. This trick had likely increased the arrow's potency beyond what any full-grown berry could.

My theory was proven true. Though his first shot only grazed the wayward fawn, its poison brought the animal to its knees. Briefly, it scurried, but its strength soon faded. The man stood solemnly over his prey, mulling thoughts through his head that I will never know. He was more ideally a warrior than any other soldier I had met.

When I returned to the village, Castillo approached me more frantically than the darting deer. His face, his eyes, and his stature all peered forward in urgency.

"Núñez! What do you make of this?"

Castillo held out his palm to reveal a stringed necklace. On its end hung a thin metal horseshoe nail and a small iron buckle, stripped unmistakably from a Spanish soldier's belt.

I stuck my hands out like a beggar. "Let me see this." Castillo handed me the necklace. "Where'd they say this was from?"

"Bearded foreigners," Castillo said.

"They're not wrong," I said. "This belt buckle is definitely Spanish military." It took me a minute, but I finally handed Castillo back his necklace. Its string was thick, strong enough to hold the tension. "You were given this permanently?" I asked.

"Yes, it's ours." Castillo smiled. "Núñez... we're almost there. After all this time."

I nodded, but could not utter a response. My head reeled. These worlds, the two spheres of my being which had developed so separately, were suddenly tethering together. The vision struck me as unnatural, and a bad taste formed in my mouth. A reluctance to return permeated my inner core. The broken land I left had finally collided with my new home.

CHAPTER 24

The Iberians Claimed

ESTEVANICO

Northern Sinaloa, Early 1536

Most indígenas thought the world was a person all its own. If there was a flowing stream, it might be the blood in the earth's veins; and if there was something small, as simple as a rock, they may consider it the very heart and soul of the world. They tried not to waste a single strip of bone, to treat every piece of the world like it meant a great deal; they considered every part as vital to the world as to their own well-being. It was all sacred; and since they lived in it, and among it, they were sacred too.

I grew to like that line of thinking. There was beauty in how the natives handled life's daily doings, and it stemmed from that belief. I doubted there had ever been a group of people sorrier to kill an animal for its meat or to rip a cornstalk from its place in the ground, not wishing to upset the earth's balance in any way.

I did not imagine this to be a very new belief. The indígenas, for as far and wide as I traveled, passed this belief on to their children generation by generation. The Iberians, who only recently had founded Nueva España, must have also realized this. But I ventured to guess it didn't make much of a difference what the natives believed; when there was a plan to follow, a real Spanish soldier could care less. Anybody in the way of expansion should suffer, they knew, regardless of their beauty and the sacredness of their lives.

I'd seen it happen in my youngest years, how the force of an empire devastates another good land. As I trekked further toward the South Sea, I saw it all again, each hellish result of conquest: the corn and beans and squash did not grow any longer, and the fields they cultivated were all burned up. Several of the villages had been toppled over, the houses burnt and the wood beams lying everywhere; across two hundred miles, I did not find a single village functioning the way it normally would. Most of the people had abandoned everything and gone into hiding, but those who were left looked very weak. They were afraid to start farming again. Most of the animals ran off, so they were unable to hunt. They ate tree bark and boiled twigs where once their stomachs were full. There was illness where once was health. I saw dead bodies on the ground; no one had time to bury them. Lots of streams and waterways ran through the region, but no indígenas stayed nearby. They died of thirst for fear of getting caught. Their blankets lay bloodstained.

The company of natives which followed us widened and winnowed at equal rates. Even as long-held followers became less comfortable with the terrible surroundings, locals sought us as a possible protection against an unenviable fate. I worried, nevertheless, that my life was instead theirs to take. At age ten, if I had been given the upper hand, how might I have reacted to a Portuguese man? I feared that the locals would conflate me for a murderer. They might exact their revenge accidentally on a fellow unfortunate soul.

I lived with fears my three Spanish companions thought impossible. They never had a motive to think from the indígena's position; past experience was my strong motive.

Our reshaped entourage decided to take us to the place where their kinsmen held refuge. We approached and became aware that nearly all the surviving natives had fled to this very spot: a raised inland mesa marked their safety. We scaled its precipitous cliff.

Castillo was wearing the necklace with the belt buckle, and he carried our only pack, which held the four sacred gourds and five emerald arrowheads given to us. I had climbed the hills with these items on my back, and only now did he offer me relief from the load. Regardless, I was grateful. Castillo had always shown his heart, though he knew not what to do with it.

"Andrés is worried the soldiers only came here temporarily," Castillo said to me. We walked some paces ahead of the rest. "He figures they might have made the trip for the sake of exploration, and that we're still far off their trail." He blinked hard from the dust in his eyes.

I scratched my beard. "He told me that too. But he's got no reason to worry."

"Why not?" he asked.

"Because, why would anybody bother to cross through a whole region, and strip it down completely, if they just wanted to explore? They're here for more."

Castillo shrugged. "I don't know... Even if it is more than just exploring, I can't see why anyone would ruin a place." Again, I noted Castillo's bleeding heart. What a blind Spaniard he was. He nearly stopped walking, as if some thought had emerged in his head. "Do you think we came here for exploration, Estevanico?"

I looked at the man—my equal in age and temperament—and I considered his question. There were many things I could say about what had driven these men: wealth, fame, superiority. Other motives came to mind. Instead of answering, I simply shook my head and kept walking.

Arriving at the mound's top, I observed how the indígenas had made their uprooted lives as tenable as possible, all without leaving a trace for their oppressors. They were impressive in their adapted skills of organization. Not all these people hailed from the same tribe, but they clearly sat and stood together as one.

Núñez, Castillo, Andrés, and I gathered in their makeshift village center, greeting the residents with somber sympathy. Primahaitu was the regional inter-tribal language, oddly enough, and we had now each learned enough to stumble through conversations. Núñez repeatedly commented on how Primahaitu was the

"Basque of the desert," which always made me chuckle; he must have believed this comparison bolstered his credibility. In no way did I think him more intelligent.

Andrés nudged me on the shoulder. "Tell them they don't have to worry about the Spaniards, Estevanico," he said. "We've got influence over what they do; tell them that." I indeed told them. The rest of the day was spent coaxing the villagers and talking with them, always forming our plan to move forward.

Another development arose unexpectedly. In the morning, a few natives who stood night-guard on the southernmost slope approached me, frightened and exhausted. "We saw the bearded men riding their horses' backs along the plain," one night-guard said. "They were close, but did not see us."

I shivered. I had always known they were close, but I never thought the day might come. "Can you take me to where you found them?" I asked the question before Andrés could nudge me to.

The night-guards hesitantly looked at one another, and I felt their trepidation. "You won't bring us to them, will you?"

"Of course not," I said.

The night-guards seemed satisfied with my response. They walked me down the southernmost slope, right onto the remnants of a troop camp. Whether carelessly or intentionally forgotten, the Spaniards had left three stakes in the ground.

"They certainly had horses here," I said, pulling the stakes out. An internal debate immediately arose as to if

I should inform my companions. They were resting, and had not followed me to the evidence. I could make the trail go cold if I liked.

I ultimately decided to impart my knowledge. There was a looming opportunity to flee, to be free in my steps. But there was an even stronger present curiosity about the future of events. I wondered, perhaps hopelessly, if the inevitable end for the indígenas might turn out differently. Here, around a few protected Spaniards, I could witness the fallout; if my expectations were subverted, I would know, and if the inevitable became true, then I was safe from a worse fate. Choosing to roam free, on the other hand, would only lead to uncertainty and death.

I showed Andrés, Núñez, and Castillo the three Spanish stakes. Their eyes all lit up. Castillo and Andrés both agreed that we should wait a day or two, wanting to rest their tired legs before pursuing these men on horseback. Núñez looked displeased.

"I feel like ending this tension," he said. "I'm going after them."

Núñez, a decade older than any of us, was a frightening force of nature when determined. To walk with him toward the Spaniards, he brought along myself and five local guides. His brisk pace led our pack.

The three stakes soon turned into an array of evidence. Every mile or so we found another stamped-out fire, pot, rope, or stray bead: every item led us closer. Hills of all sizes walled our path and kept out the breeze. It felt as if the plateaus narrowed our focus. Thirty miles in a single day is what we went, the most intense march I'd ever been on; nighttime arrived under some leafless trees, and I still was sweating.

I crashed hard on the dirt; Núñez fell not long afterward. My body was exhausted. Núñez's mind raced, however, and he turned to speak. "Estevanico, can I confide something in you?"

"Yes, of course," I said, curious.

The charred Spaniard sighed and frowned. "It's been on my mind for years, and I've tried to tell myself it's not true. But seeing these stakes and pots and the belt buckle necklace, I'm finally having to face it: I don't feel like going back. Not yet, at least."

My eyebrows raised. "You don't? I mean, it seems like you're the most adamant in tracking them."

"I am," he said. "Though it's only to ease the anticipation. I'm hoping my mind might change when I see the Spaniards face to face. But for now, I'm dreading it." Núñez cleared his throat. "Estevanico, you can't tell Castillo or Andrés this; they'll think less of me."

I reassured him. "I won't, Núñez. You can rest well in that." I shut my eyes, wanting to drift off.

Núñez still had one last grievance to air. "I really enjoyed my life, you know." He gazed up, as if his confession was more to heaven than to me. "I was completely free to do as I pleased. I saw things daily which topped my best days in Spain. People thought of me highly. I finally became a legend; I even had an excuse to stay, too, with that young man Lope stuck on the island." Núñez smiled a heartfelt grin. It quickly fell. "But then I complicated things. My patrons had to pick between me and their good relations with neighbors. I had to leave my life. When Lope chose to stay, and I kept moving, I may have made a mistake." He now looked down at me. "The Iberians can't know I enjoyed my life, Estevanico. They'll crucify me."

I nodded, unsettled. If even Núñez felt afraid, then maybe I was underestimating my own oppressors.

I desired sleep more than anything else. All day, when sleep was not an option, I searched for something to eat, and when I found something I saved it, waiting until the night to eat and rest.

The five natives stamped out the morning fire as we moved along, a precaution they considered necessary; Núñez was already on his feet, speaking to them with his limited vocabulary. Soon enough I was standing with him, for a distinct sound had jolted me awake.

"It's a horse," Núñez said.

I agreed. "They aren't far."

Our local guides remained where they were, hoping to preserve their safety.

Núñez and I loaded our few items into packs, marching out toward the neighing steed. Núñez had me follow a winding stream, which he claimed any soldier would think to do; he felt confident this was their route.

An hour passed and his confidence proved correct.

A horse, the one who had been neighing, stood in its magnificence beside a dying tree. Someone had tied it to a stake for fear that the tree would topple. Three other horses waited silently in another leafless grove, each a different shining color. I hadn't seen a horse in ages. But I could hardly focus on that alone. I saw another face, a human face near that of the horses. He reclined his body against a stump, eating the last remnants of a midday meal from a rusted metal pot. There was a rosary tied onto his shirt strings, and you could tell he was a Spaniard by the way he kept his hair. His shirt was clean, almost completely white, and his pants did not have a scratch in their fabric. A black belt ran around his waist to keep his pants from falling; the belt held a sheathed sword, and I saw a musket on the ground nearby. There wasn't a thing about him that wasn't Spanish: not his clothes, not his features, and I'm sure not even his name. He had a tanned face, a short beard, over-exuberant clothing, and a lack of earrings, paints, and lean physique. I hadn't seen a man with such Iberian traits in nine years. My accompanying Spaniards no longer looked like this man; their beards were growing long, their shirts were missing, and their pants had been discarded. They didn't have his same rosary, or sword, or musket, or metal pot. This man sat in full Spanish glory, a contrast to the failure of his kinsmen, my companions. Three other fine Iberians waited behind him on their horses for him to finish his food. It felt a very strange phenomenon to see this manner of foreigner endure in the indígena's homeland.

The soldier stopped scooping from his pot, meeting the eyes of myself and my striking companion.

Núñez looked at him for a while, as did I, and we looked at the other three too. No one said anything. They must have been shocked to witness a seemingly Spanish native and a naked Moor, walking together in the land of the indís. They were clearly startled.

A few minutes passed, and still no one said anything. The man had set aside his pot, and the horse did not neigh like before; every man's mouth stayed wide open. I could hear a fly streaming across the air. I could feel my heart beating for a way out.

Núñez visibly rummaged through his thoughts. "I don't think you could ever know how pleased I am to see you," he said.

The four horsemen simply stared at him for a while longer.

"This must be the guard post." Núñez peered around at the camp almost magically. "I'm just wondering where your captain might be... Who's your head-in command?"

Still, the Spaniards could not answer.

"Do you know where we are right now?" Núñez asked. "We've been gone so long that I'm not sure exactly where this is, at least in relation to Nueva España. I don't even know the date."

The man in the front slowly began to react. "This is a guard post," he said. "We're about, I'd say, seventy-five miles from Culiacán. Our troop has been doing work around here for a while."

Núñez nodded, tears beginning to well. "Great. And who's your captain?" he asked.

"Alcaraz," said the cavalryman. "His name's Alcaraz, and he's in the main camp, just a walk south."

The men said they were sorry they didn't have any clothes for us, and that the corn pot was their last ration, so we'd have to wait for other food. Perhaps they would also provide me with chains.

Just a minute, they said, and we'll head back to main camp.

PART THREE

AMERICANO

CHAPTER 25

Captain Alcaraz

ALVAR NÚÑEZ

With the Spanish Cavalry, 1536

Captain Alcaraz did not have the same well-kept features of his outpost guards. His beard was scraggly, his shirt dotted with mud stains, and his pants slightly torn; a knife hilt extended from his tarnished belt and a broken crossbow lay by his side. But even the captain, himself weathered, was shocked to see a man so far flung from any thread of civilized life. The silence that came over him lasted quite a while.

When he finally spoke, the heat of day had reached its height, and he didn't have much tolerance for questioning. He asked about how I came to arrive at his camp, along with a few other points of interest. I told him that Estevanico and I wanted to get to Nueva España as soon as possible.

The three of us—Alcaraz, Estevanico, and myself—sat around a lifeless fire-pit; no one ate, since nothing had been offered.

Alcaraz had sweat collecting beneath his arms. "We've still got some work to manage here," the Captain said. "We can take you to San Miguel, but it will take a while." He wiped the perspiration off his forehead. An armored hat, the kind a Spanish soldier feels he must wear for its impression, added a large weight to his head.

"That's understandable," I said, clearing my throat. "I do need something from you though, Captain."

Alcaraz finally took off his hat and tossed it aside. His hair looked damp. "What do you need?"

"I need you to write a document."

"What for?" he asked briskly.

"I want to know what day it is," I said. "Me, and the Moor here, have been stranded a very long time... we lost track of the date."

"It's March 19th."

My ears perked up at hearing the day's date, positively, for the first time in years. "Thank you," I said. "I would also like the document to say how you found us, and what we look like right now. All the other details, too."

He moved the strands of hair off his forehead. "You want evidence?"

I spoke confidently. "Yes, I do."

Captain Alcaraz raised his brow. "You figure that people aren't going to believe you?" He pointed to my chest, where the intruding outline of my ribs stuck out. "They'll have evidence enough."

Estevanico smiled, trying to deflect the Captain's statement. I, however, didn't think a document was too much to ask for. "I'm sure you're right," I said. "But I do still want that document."

Captain Alcaraz took a moment to consider. A red ant started to crawl its way up his leg, but he quickly crushed it with an adjacent finger. The Captain finally nodded, caving in to my request. He showed me a completed document, with the date and all the details, and I told him it sufficed. I then posed a question about food, but Alcaraz said his men also felt starved; the natives weren't tending to the fields anymore, for whatever reason. He complained that the indís had fled and his troop couldn't find them, and I watched Estevanico's face turn sick with distaste. I too found it unnerving that the soldiers' should complain about the lack of food when they themselves had undeniably scorched the fields.

I informed the Captain that we still had two more Spaniards some miles back, Castillo and Dorantes, possibly making their way here. The Captain, considering our desperate condition, thought it odd that we should split, especially if it left the other two to an uncertain fate. His face turned stern. "Were there indís where you left them? It's possible they kept your friends company while you went off looking for us," he said. "Considering how you were guided here by natives yourselves, I'd guess that's not far from the truth." Alcaraz did not try to hide what he was really asking. He had a mission to achieve, no matter the methods involved. It just so happened that Alcaraz, like most other Spanish soldiers I knew, favored an attitude of brutality. His sword, crossbow, and armored hat all told a story. Alcaraz must have suspected Estevanico and myself of standing in the way of his gloried achievement.

I considered my answer. If I lied completely about our following's existence, then our credibility to speak on their behalf would be diminished. If I told him the full extent of my native entanglement, however, my own ability to reacclimate would be forever halted.

I answered him. "Not that I know of. They might have come after we left, though. Who knows."

CHAPTER 26

A Bad Deed

ALONSO DEL CASTILLO

En Route to Culiacán, April 1536

Núñez and Estevanico approached us with what looked like several Spaniards.

I never expected to see them so soon, so it took me a while to make sure my eyes were not mistaken. They walked closer, and closer, and in time I knew it was true, that these men really had come from Nueva España, with Iberian blood flowing through their veins. Dorantes' tears could not be contained, and I also cried out in thanks, for we had been found.

Alvar Núñez soon unsettled my excitement, however. "Captain Alcaraz caught me in a lie," he said to me and Dorantes. Núñez had taken us aside, out of earshot from the Spanish soldiers. "I tried to pretend there weren't more natives with us, but he insisted on taking us back to you firsthand. If I had it my way, Estevanico and I would have come earlier with a warning."

"I'm sure it's fine," Dorantes said. "They're with us; he can see they're treating us well. Alacaraz isn't going to do anything bad."

"I wouldn't be so sure," Núñez said.

This statement struck me, and the following weeks only served further discouragement.

By this point in the year—springtime—the desert's few trees had bloomed and the sun's true heat started to show its face; while there were rivers and streams scattered about, even water couldn't seem to ease a man's dry throat. Captain Alcaraz didn't let dryness distract him though, as his thoughts seemed deeply engaged in scouring his surroundings. "Tell them they've done a fine job getting you this far," he said to Núñez, "but that there's no further need for their guidance."

"Will do." Núñez turned to the strong Susola woman from our initial guides. He spoke to her in a tongue from much farther north, not the local Primahaitu; instead of relaying the captain's words, Núñez shared his own advice. "Whatever he tells you, do not leave. We can only guarantee your safety for as long as you're with us. They may ask to take your supplies; everyone should comply with this. It is not ideal, but I do believe this is the best decision available."

The Susola woman solemnly nodded, then she spread Núñez's words to the varied peoples who inhabited the mound haven. A consensus grew that his advice should be followed. "Besides," the Susola guide said, reporting back to us, "we don't leave our guests until they're safely in the homes of another."

Captain Alcaraz responded with a request for the indígenas' supplies. He did not like their refusal to leave, and so viewed this payment as just compensation. Our followers and the locals handed over all their hides, blankets, and bows to Alcaraz's men without a struggle. They even unearthed the corn which they hid beneath the ground in clay pots. Even the fiercely-critical Maliacone woman handed over her prized possessions. While Alcaraz's Spanish troop were about seventy strong, these people who had supported us ranked far greater in number. They could have fought for what was theirs, but they desired peace.

We trekked for several days, and in that time I spoke with Captain Alcaraz. I sought out information on how well the Iberians in Nueva España knew this region and its tribes; in return, I told him little, as I simply wanted a gauge. During one such conversation, Alcaraz let important information slip.

"Culiacán, the town you're taking us to," I had asked, "what administration is it under?"

He answered. "It's in New Galicia, one of the outermost sections of the colony. When we bring the natives in to labor, they'll likely remain around there."

My eyebrows raised, but I faked a subdued reaction. "I see... thank you. I've never had the chance to learn how the colony is divided."

I immediately rushed to the Susola guide with this revelation, but she was not surprised to hear this. "Of course," she said. "We know that's what they intend for us. Can't you see everyone's heads hung low?" Hearing the dejection in her voice, I looked around at my sorry company and knew I had to take action.

"Alcaraz," I said, marching back up to the Captain. "There's no way you're bringing these people in for labor. They have brought us to you of their own free will, and chosen nothing but peace and hospitality."

Captain Alcaraz shrugged. "I don't know what to tell you. They're not going back to their old homes, that's for sure. That region is going to be absorbed into New Galicia when we're done there. They won't have any other option."

I scoffed. "You obviously haven't spent much time around the indígenas. They can survive nearly anywhere; they don't need to labor for food or your security." A thought sprang into my head. "Besides, you're missing an opportunity, Alcaraz. Instead of burning the fields and relocating the only people who know how to tend them, you could be making an arrangement: restored land for food tributes. Your men would never go hungry and these people would never have to worry about losing their home. You're working against yourself."

"Don't pin it all on me," he said. "My strategy comes from the top down. And it's a time-proven strategy." Alcaraz gave me a patronizing smile. "But you know what? I'll let you put your plans in place; a long-lost man like you probably has an insight or two I'm missing. I just need to hear it from their mouths first. If they want an arrangement, then let's make it official."

"You want it written?" I asked. "Like a treaty?"

He looked over at Núñez. "Your friend here wanted his own reflection in writing, so I don't see how it's too much to ask."

"Fine," I said. "We'll strike out a deal. I'll interpret for them."

He shook his head. "No thanks; I've got my own. Bring the indís to speak with him in Primahaitu."

Assenting, I gathered the leaders of the assorted tribes in our midst. Hardly any were chiefs or elders, as we had assembled an odd mix of followers with no clear structure. I told the more leader-like personalities about the proposal, and they instantly had negative reactions.

"No, we're not going to leave you without assurances that you're in safe hands," the Susola woman said. "You're as foreign to us as these soldiers, but you are also as different from them as we are."

The Maliacone woman nodded in agreement. "Trust is earned by more than a piece of paper. These men have done nothing to prove they are trustworthy."

I accurately relayed this reaction to Captain Alcaraz.

"They don't even think of you as Spaniards?" Alcaraz asked me. "That's why they don't want to leave you with us?"

"Partially," I said. "They have personal concerns, as well."

"God, what a mess." Alcaraz chuckled to himself. "Take my interpreter with you; his name's Cebreros. You tell them, Don Castillo, that this is the best assurance they'll get. You make it clear that this is their only other option."

The 'Don' of 'Don Castillo' had clearly been meant to sting my pride.

Red with frustration, I led Cebreros the interpreter back over to the leaders among our entourage. "Go ahead, Castillo," Cebreros said. "Explain to them why they should agree, and let's see what they say." Cebreros, a bookkeeper who had learned broken Primahaitu through manufactured means, was ordering me, a survivor taught by necessity, on the manner by which I should speak to my companions. I felt incensed, but maintained my calm.

"I understand your concerns," I said to the indígena representatives. "Trust is indeed made up of far more than simple promises. But these men are my countrymen. Myself and the other three sun children are in safe hands. As for your own sake, you also should not worry. Once they sign a treaty, my countrymen do not break their words. Signing papers is how they assure their honesty when there is no chance to prove through action. I believe you all should come to a written agreement."

The assembled leaders convened for a moment and then responded. "We find it strange that your countrymen accept papers in lieu of actions. There is always a chance for action to prove or disprove what has been agreed in words," the Susola guide said. Her serious expression soon turned into a smile. "However, we understand that these are your countrymen. If you are so sure of your comfort, then we feel at peace with leaving you. As for ourselves, we will come to an agreement with these men. If they, as foreigners like you, might have the same capacity for healing and trustworthiness that you have shown us, then we should hope that their promise is truthful. Even if they have displayed otherwise, we do believe your word, Castillo. So please take us to meet with these men."

I walked with Cebreros and the native leaders to where Alcaraz was resting. By this point, Núñez, Dorantes, and Estevanico had come to stand near me as the two parties worked out an agreement. Over an hour passed, but a consensus was reached; I read the document to make sure it reflected the decisions. It indeed was accurate: our native followers would be allowed to re-inhabit their homes without disturbance, provided they monthly delivered a set amount of food to the outposts of New Galicia. This amount was not indulgent, but only enough to aid the Spanish soldiers in their subsistence. I sighed away my nagging stress. I had at last spared my loving companions from further troubles.

The hundreds of people who had followed us said their goodbyes. We gave each man, woman, and child a final, heartfelt parting before seeing them on their way. As I reflected, a realization became ever clearer. They had truly been very good to us.

Núñez looked displeased. "I'm worried about ruining their trust in us," he said. "I'm worried about them in general. What if they can't produce enough crops on those burnt fields?"

"Stop worrying," Dorantes said. "They've got an entire country with enough resources; even if they can't make their old homes fertile, then they'll find another place to live. They'll be fine no matter where they get pushed to." Núñez reluctantly nodded in response.

Alvar Núñez, the former soldier, had aged terribly, and his thoughts emerged at a much slower pace. But his eyes could not have seemed more alive. Their brightness contrasted the rather silent manner of our new company: the four naked survivors and the group of fully-adorned fighting men.

At last Captain Alcaraz broke the silence. "I must turn back to my post, as must most of my men," he said. "I won't be personally taking you to Nueva España. But Cebreros, my interpreter and closest aide, will lead you in a dispatch to the town of San Miguel de Culiacán. It's less than a fortnight off, and he knows the way."

"What keeps you from coming with us, Captain?" Núñez asked.

Alcaraz straightened his back. "I have unfinished business. Too much time spent going into town and my work will never get done."

"Of course." Núñez frowned.

It felt obvious to me that Captain Alcaraz considered our presence a liability. Though his entire troop numbered near seventy, just six soldiers were assigned to accompany us and Cebreros. Our departure was as hasty and unceremonious as our arrival had been.

I'd like to say that the cold reception from my countrymen bothered me; however, I knew these men were society's most crotchety. If the hard-boiled Alvar Núñez of several years ago was a metric for the Spanish soldier's disposition, then this cold reception was standard. Better recognition surely awaited us in the town.

On our trek, I tried to daydream about Nueva España. I pushed myself to think of bathing in hot water, wearing new clothing, and viewing paintings of beautiful women. Perhaps I would hear professional melodies played from thick Italian parchment; however, the notes of the lyre presently escaped me. Instead, the reed-flute rang out loudly in my head. I frequently paused my musings to count the number of fallen trees or to observe the six Spanish soldiers sweating through their shirts. Every dry forest stretch proved denser, enough that we were soon separated from any flowing streams. Now, not only did our food become scarce, but our water also; I fought off thoughts of its sweet taste. Myself and the other three survivors had gone as much as four days without water before; we knew how to slow our bodies into acceptance. But the surrounding soldiers, two days dehydrated, looked sickly and scared. They didn't know how to adapt. They couldn't halt their thoughts, or shift shamelessly into survival. They didn't have the means to move on without a stream flowing by their side.

Núñez stopped in his tracks. "Why didn't we follow the stream?"

His question caught us all by surprise. Cebreros, the captain's aide, turned back. He asked what my friend meant.

Núñez had a stiff, stern face. "Why didn't we follow the stream, the one leading southeast, from the moment we split with the troop?"

Cebreros' leaner figure matched his balding head. "The stream?"

"Yes, the stream!" Núñez said again. "Why are we in this forest, instead of following the streams out into open fields?"

Cebreros looked confused, a little bothered. "This is the way to San Miguel; this is the path to town. What on Earth is wrong with you?"

Núñez looked up into the interpreter's eyes. "I've been watching the sun for years," he said. "I know which way is east, and which is west, and I know the north from the south almost as well. If you think you can trick me, which you are mistakenly doing right now, then you'd better have a good excuse for it."

"Excuse me?" Cebreros said.

Núñez leaned in closer. "You're taking us north... Why are we going north?"

Of all things, I hadn't been paying attention to direction. The soldiers knew the way to Culiacán, so why should I have worried which way the sun set? But Alvar Núñez always remained on his toes. Now that he had brought this strange detail to my attention, I could see that we were in fact heading north, unnecessarily angling away from Nueva España.

Cebreros seemed fidgety and affronted to answering. "It's a precaution." His face reddened. "We can't have you running into trouble with the natives; the forested route is the best way to avoid them."

Núñez pressed his weight forward. He was physically tired, but was energetically fixated on his questioning. "What do you mean, 'precaution'?"

"Captain Alcaraz didn't want you reaching the natives out this far," Cebreros said. "Who's to say how they'll react when we walk by."

Núñez shook his head, angry.

For a while, no one spoke, and Núñez kept shaking his head. "That's not why you're taking us this way," he finally said. He rubbed his forehead, and I could feel his internal strain.

"Pardon?"

"That's not the real reason." Núñez clenched his hands and shifted his weight. "You know what you've been doing, why you brought us out this far... Alcaraz and his men, they've got their horses, and their swords, and their muskets. You know what the plan is."

Cebreros stood silent.

"Massacre," Núñez said. "He's slaughtering all of them." Alvar Núñez glared with sober madness at the captain's aide. He choked away a strange internal cry, then contained himself. He spoke again. "They're not going to make it home. Not back to their fields, and nowhere near the four of us, that's for sure. You're never going to let us stop it."

Cebreros stared back, now pale.

"But it's too late!" Núñez's knees were shaking as he pointed an accusing finger. "They're already dead! You won't even let us see the corpses!"

I stood in disbelief. Estevanico, Dorantes, and the six soldiers were watching him too; our movement had slowed to a standstill, yet his knees were still shaking, ready to buckle from an unseen weight. Núñez knew, as I soon realized, that there would be no chance to right this wrong.

The women who delivered us and the children who played, they all lay dead with their men at the foothills they called home. Whether they were a guiding Susola or a questioning Maliacone, it made no difference. These scores of people had been slaughtered by the horse-riders who shared my blood. My promise for their safety died alongside them.

CHAPTER 27

The Magistrate of San Miguel

MELCHOR DÍAZ

The Outskirts of Culiacán, Late April 1536

"The sheer magnitude of what you've done is rather impressive, I hope you know," I said. My boots felt tight, but I kept them on. I wanted to remind these men what professionalism looked like. "Last night, hearing your ordeal, it didn't please me to learn I may have had a hand in making it worse for you."

There was a silence. They were tired, spent. A pregnant pause filled the room as a blanket which smothered any potential response.

Four men with startling features sat before me in the tile-roofed building. We were miles outside the town of San Miguel, where I had met them just the night before, and I had heard how they had crawled out from hell's depths to make it here. According to them, our dispatch had not eased their struggles in any way; in fact, the troop took the four on a dangerous offbeat track, all to spite their native connections. Today, these men waited with tired spirits, still poorly accommodated. Hearing of their struggles had put me to shame, at least in my present mind, and I thanked God for bringing them back.

The eldest man tapped his fingers on the hardwood floor. His back reclined against the wall, an outside light reflecting off his hair's bald patches. His beard was entirely torn out in some places, with no signs of growth to come. What hair he did have was singed to its very ends. The startling sight of his skin-pressed skeleton drew my attention all the more: a butchered head did not feel so out of place on a withered body.

Next to him, staring without purpose, was the man whose bright hair could not diminish his blatant punctures. Every scar, dotting him here and there, told a different miserable story. There was still strength, it seemed, in his broad shoulders, but the contracted torso and misshapen knees which followed appeared to have taken the weight of each step with lessening fortitude. Swollen could not begin to describe what Hell had wrought on him.

He cleared a line of gravel from his throat. "Do you have water?" he asked.

I looked over. The cup I kept nearly full lay beside my desk. "Yes, I have some here." I grabbed the water and brought it to his side of the room.

He took generous swallows, stopping for a breath and returning to drink. It was a large cup.

Another of the four men watched him drink without a visible reaction. From a standing position, he seemed to envy the cool lapse in thirst. Why he did not ask for his own water, I could plainly see, but why he did not sit, I could not understand. He was an obvious Moor, a slave from the African coast whose years of servitude might have numbered near the years of his life. I noticed him shift his weight, at last, but the simple warning in his brain cautioned him not to let his brawny legs rest. No one had told him not to.

"Why don't you sit down?" I said.

The Moor looked at me, and then, gradually, he allowed himself to sit beside the others.

I decided to continue. "When you expressed your plans to leave by noon today, it was no shock. Honestly, I too would want to get into town as quickly as I could if I had gone through your ordeal. But I must ask you, however selfish it may seem, to stay for only a while longer..."

The man sitting farthest left stared in my direction. His eyes, green, with streaks of hazel, were seriously strained. Dark yellow clouds formed in the whites around his pupils, and I noticed thin lines of crimson streaked throughout. He wore a necklace with a sword belt buckle and a horseshoe nail laced in the front. It must have been some native trinket.

"You want us to stay?" he asked. If he had rested better, his statement would probably have revealed his full frustration.

"Yes," I said. "I would be overjoyed if you men stayed here, and then again in San Miguel, for just a couple weeks, maybe a month."

The man on the left grabbed his head, eyes now closed, as if some migraine had just struck him. He didn't like my request. Neither did the eldest man with singed hair, for he shook his head.

"We would love to do your little favors," he said, leaning forward. "But unless there's a good reason, Melchor Díaz, I'd very much like to go into town and away from your Captain and his marauders."

I nodded, sympathetic. "Honestly, I don't pretend to know what you're feeling... Núñez, is it?"

"Yes, that's me."

"Well, Núñez, I wouldn't hold any of you back if I didn't have the best reasons. And after hearing what you had to say about that patrol..."

He interrupted. "Alcaraz."

"Yes, Captain Alcaraz," I said, taking a heavy breath. "After hearing what he's done, I've come to the realization that you four are the best suited to fixing our problems. Nobody else has ever spent so much time in indígena country, and nobody else understands how to control them so well. If you stayed here, and worked with me for just a while, then maybe we can actually have a conversion, or lots of conversions. Maybe we can stop the soldiers from thinking they need to disrupt everything. We can meet our goals in other ways."

Núñez nodded. "It's a good thought, really. But the people who had any connection with us were killed. All that influence you speak of has been wiped out."

The man with the necklace agreed. "Núñez is right. We can't do a thing if there isn't anyone who'll listen."

"I hear what you're saying," I said. "But that in itself is exactly the problem: no one else knows how to handle the indís. And what good does it do anyone to have the land rot away, and the gold, the silver, and the food go to waste? They're the only ones who know how to tend these fields; but still, no one thinks of that. They choose to inhibit the locals in their own specialty, when they should instead be making a beneficial arrangement."

They gave me some blank stares, though I certainly now had their attention.

"You four are the first people I've met who can help me change this," I said. "There's an opportunity out here, one they're letting slide right through our fingers. The apple cart of ignorance hasn't yet tipped over; but I think you men have the knowledge enough to push it. In a few weeks, you won't see the same blatant disregard for progress, not in my jurisdiction at least. I can promise you that."

CHAPTER 28

Proselytizer

ESTEVANICO

San Miguel de Culiacán, May 1536

One bad solution had been replaced by another. This time, however, my three companions did not have the wherewithal to recognize the mistake.

To Melchor Díaz's credit, he knew that land, safety, and bodily freedom were parts of life the indígenas cared about. Also to his credit, he had a kind enough heart not to manipulate these factors to the natives' detriment—at least not actively. Where Melchor Díaz went wrong, then, was in his philosophy on culture and the freedom of the mind. He believed these traits should be in line with the Iberian standard.

His primary motive was quickly revealed to be conversion. Melchor Díaz was clearly a pious man, yes, but he also believed a common faith to be the only means by which his much-needed progress could be achieved.

The indígenas should first adopt a Catholic disposition, then all else would fall into place. Their homes, lives, and bodies would once again be theirs if they simply changed themselves from the inside out. For all the four of us had supposedly learned, we were bound to be his agents in this endeavor.

None of my companions saw the problems with this plan. Castillo, God love him, even took a liking to the process; he had just spent years going through an extraordinary conversion experience, and he now deeply desired the whole world to share in this splendor. Outward displays of religiosity covered his inner insecurities. Melchor Díaz had given him the spark which made this expression possible.

"I first would like you to give testimony to the natives being housed near San Miguel," Díaz said. "They've had a rough time recently; like I've told you, my administration is rather new here, as is the administration as a whole. A few unnoticed soldiers got carried away, as you're well aware they can do. They took over a village, and had their way with these women; they also brought in the men, hoping to hinder the option for retribution. I've taken care of the matter, but the natives are still in our care. I think they'd be well served to hear the Gospel before getting sent back home."

We four, on our years-long journey, had never fully converted a single soul. There was no evidence of a conversion because conversion had not been our goal. Perhaps some people might have gone gladly to Christ if our agenda had been to proselytize through our healing and blessings. Núñez could have easily won some souls after he raised a man from the dead. Castillo had briefly flirted with the idea, but had felt bad about it in the moment. It was now through outside encouragement that his guiltiness subsided.

The San Miguel boarding houses were a despicable site. The Spanish had not cared for their prisoners; they had even left the women bare and uncleaned, as if to shame them for the crimes of their attackers. Our first priority was thus to walk them to our current lodgings and out of these squalid conditions. I felt so sorry for the women that I gave them my sacred gourd; it was only item I had personally owned since enslavement.

Because our current lodgings were in fact in one of Melchor Díaz's homes, we needed to address the conversion topic before we dared to allow these women to use his comfortable surroundings. My companions thus began to proselytize. Castillo became their source of revelatory excitement, while Andrés imparted the Bible stories he remembered from childhood. Núñez wavered between these two, preaching deep theology with the confidence of a man who had likely never read scripture. I, in an effort to balance these overwhelming subjects, opted to tell these indígenas the practical truth they were looking for.

I opened with a question. "What are your names?" I asked. The women, who looked frightened, bothered, confused, and bored by these foreign ideologies, were certainly not expecting a question. The Iberians never asked them many questions.

They paused a moment. Finally, they told me their names.

I shared my own name, then asked them another question. "What do you believe?"

The women made a couple comments to each other, but a response was eventually mustered: they believed in a heavenly man named Aguar, who had created the earth and given every stretch of water its flow.

I asked them how they knew about him.

The women from the boarding house looked to be from the same tribe, although they had no belongings or markings to suggest it. "Our fathers and grandfathers told us about Aguar when we were little," one said. "The earliest of our ancestors saw him, and they always knew to pass on the tales about his great deeds. We, too, passed them on to our children." At this, her disposition dropped, but she continued. "When we recently heard about you, and all your great deeds, we were astounded; but we always remember that none is as great as Aguar, for no one else created the earth and all its beauty."

I nodded in response.

For nearly a half hour, I listened to what they had to say; every time they finished telling me about something, I would ask them another question, but only about them and their beliefs. Question after question, response after response, it was more and more clear that God was not all that distant from Aguar, at His core. As far as the span of native beliefs went, Aguar was surprisingly similar to what the Iberians prescribed. Luckily for these women, their conversion would be much less invasive than most. Not that it ever was truly a benign process. I knew that all too well.

"You know something," I finally said. "We believe in Aguar too... we just go about it a bit differently."

That shocked the women very much, especially after hearing so much about that "God" fellow from my companions.

Seeing this, I explained to them everything. The Son of Aguar came and died for their sins, and he lived again. They were receptive, interested with the Son of Aguar, as if the few remaining pieces of their spiritual lives could be unlocked. Salvation, sin, grace, love, all became concepts they took to heart, codes they could live by. I was surprised by how open they were. They heard from me the history of a man living halfway across the world, more than a thousand years ago, and they were able to take his message into the fold of their lives, just like I had been forced to do. I saw the most earnest faces I had ever seen, and likely will ever see. The Spaniards will forever fail until they learn to listen and respond. Even still, they likely won't see success.

By the time we arrived at Melchor Díaz's home, I gave the women a very important additional piece of instruction. "You can't call him Aguar anymore," I said. "Foreigners don't understand. They think you're talking about someone else." Their brows were furrowed, listening carefully. "When the foreign Christians are around, and even when you're alone, you should call him God. There are other ways of calling him Aguar, but they're almost the same. The men who are here just don't seem to care about that fact."

The women said they must be pretty dumb if they couldn't understand a simple thing like that.

I nodded, agreeing that the Iberians were surprisingly dense most of the time. "But you also have to know," I continued, "that believing in the Son of Aguar and calling him Jesus means you can go back to your homes freely, and replant the fields you left behind. The Christians, if they see a church you build and the crosses you carry instead of bows, will be astonished, and treat you like friends. They will go into your huts and eat with you like any other peoples, and after a while, they will leave you alone. Even the man who lives here will let you have warmth and comfort."

My stomach churned and I felt a cold sting inside.

In saying this, I promised them survival. It was the same promise I received from the Dorantes family when I abandoned Islam. The same promise was also made to the people who had guided me here. It was a sweet, empty promise to hear. I simply hoped that for these current few it wouldn't be a broken one.

We never did have much control over what was and wasn't broken. We just had to live without letting these troubles break our spirits.

CHAPTER 29

Dinner with Hernando

ALVAR NÚÑEZ

San Miguel de Culiacán, May 10ᵗʰ, 1536

"Hernando Cortés will be staying with us for the next few days," Melchor Díaz had said. "I have some last arrangements to attend to outside of town, but I'll be back tomorrow. You'll have to play the hosts tonight." He turned to Estevanico. "I'm not positive if your presence will offend him, but it's best to err on the side of caution. Do you mind travelling with me today, Estevanico?" The Moroccan obliged, of course, and prepared to leave with Melchor Díaz that afternoon.

Díaz lent us some of his clothes for the occasion and went on his way. His home was impeccable. The outward tiled shingles invited the eyes and feet into a hall of open, decadent arrangement. The food had been cooked by Díaz's housemaid; the table was set by his wife. I made sure that my beard was cut short, wanting the exposed patches to blend in more believably; my appearance met an acceptable standard, I thought. Nevertheless, so much time had passed since my last encounter with a Spaniard of high regard. It was anyone's guess as to whether I would make a good impression.

Hernando Cortés, my greatest living inspiration, sat at the table next to me. Castillo was seated across, and Andrés Dorantes beside him.

Señora Díaz finished setting the table. "Well, I'm off to retire for the night," she said. "I hope you enjoy the meal." We thanked her for the food, knowing full well she'd be awake for another hour or so in solitude.

Hernando Cortés finished his bite of pork chop, leaning slightly back to savor its taste. He then began our conversation. "As I hear it, you men have had quite the past few years," he said. Cortés waited, hoping this would be enough to prompt us to speak. But I could not think of anything. I might have said *Yes, we have* or *You've heard correctly*, but they seemed like useless pleasantries.

Castillo, in true fashion, broke the silence. He looked less presentable than both Dorantes and myself, and certainly less than Cortés. His skeletal physique was out of place at the dinner table. "It has been an experience," Castillo said. "And not always the best one, Don Cortés, as you can imagine."

"Please, call me Hernando," Cortés said. "But of course. You've seen a lot of men die, and I would fail in trying to compare your struggles to my own. Where you were is a much different arena."

Hernando Cortés was shorter than I imagined. I was also surprised by his respect for our experiences. Had he not also seen many men die? Perhaps his traumas had felt much more like a war than ours; he had spent years in advance, and I had spent years in retreat. Pains in retreat were undoubtedly greater. Something in his last statement, though, that we were in *a much different arena*, felt veiled and measured. Watching Cortés speak from the side, I uniquely saw his thoughts in formation; his eyes were tools of presentation, and his real gaze had moved to the periphery. What his addressee Castillo saw was intentional, and what was left unseen remained Cortés' own. His true thoughts resided in the whites of his eyes.

"I also can't assume to know what you've gone through," Castillo said. "But I imagine your experiences must have been somewhat like our own. Personally, I never fully adjusted." He laughed, trying to build a sense of congeniality. Cortés smiled in kind. "But it wasn't all bad." Castillo stopped laughing. "They certainly weren't all bad."

Andrés Dorantes interjected. "Hernando, speaking for all of us, we're very interested to hear about what you've been doing this past decade." He gave a hearty laugh. "We've fallen behind on current events, you see."

Cortés joined him in laughter. "No, you've been shaping current events! A much higher calling. Besides, I haven't been up to anything new. Largely administrative work. I doubt there's much I could tell you about myself that you don't know already."

"Ah, but that's all legend," I said. "How are we to know what's true without your take on the matter?"

Cortés turned his intentional gaze toward me for the first time. I nearly choked on my words. I momentarily panicked; I hadn't really thought about the comment, how reducing his life to a tall tale might offend him. I almost expected him to lash out. Instead, Cortés broke into a thin smile. "That's a wise policy," he said. "Unless you're talking to someone who wants to be a legend. In that case, their version is only meant to confuse. It's best to combine the two stories."

"I hadn't thought of that," Andrés Dorantes said, his chewed rice still to the side of his mouth. "So what is your version, Hernando?"

Hernando Cortés burst into another bout of laughter. It felt quite unprompted. Dorantes and Castillo chuckled in camaraderie, though they did not know what for. I rested my fork on the edge of my plate, ready to hear his answer.

"Where to begin!" Cortés said. "Iberia? I could take you all the way back home. But very few stories start best at the beginning. You're all Spaniards, I assume?"

Castillo swallowed hard. "Yes, we are." He motioned to himself. "I've been meaning to visit my parents in Salamanca again. But I'm not looking forward to another trans-Atlantic."

"Hmm, yes," Cortés said, not as joyous as before. "Best to put that off until you feel your time here has passed."

"Coming from you, that advice is no surprise," I said, beaming. "You don't seem like one to turn back... You burnt your ships, after all!" I hoped to make up for my last indiscretion with this indirect compliment. It felt a bit odd, though; I had not considered currying favor this actively since my military days.

Hernando Cortés gave a meek smile, with somewhat of a blush. He had undoubtedly heard this before, so his response must have been a repeatable one. "I'd speak on that, but perhaps I enjoy the legend too much."

I chuckled for the first time that night.

Andrés Dorantes responded rather abruptly. "Your legend certainly has taken off. It led our poor Governor to his grave, trying to leave the ships like you had."

Cortés' eyes lit up in the front. This brightness quickly moved to the sides, to the whites of his eyes; I saw the light wavering there. "Oh, really?" he finally said, measured.

"Yes," Dorantes said, "he even backtracked, having us build new rafts. He wanted us all to get here safely."

Cortés' eyes now shone in full. He lost his feigned demeanor. "Interesting," he said, almost to himself. "I'm surprised he decided to head this way."

I stared very carefully at Hernando Cortés. His adventurous acumen was admirable; he was a figure who had earned every facet of his status. But, so far, all I had heard from him alarmed me. Against all nostalgia, I determined he could not be trusted.

Castillo interjected immediately, listening to the wrong parts of his words. "Yes, I would've thought to look a little longer for gold, too. But you must understand, Hernando, we were beginning to starve. And it was demoralizing; the region and people there were highly impoverished. Further South and West they were much better off, we soon found out."

Cortés cleared his throat and sat up. "Of course, it's never best to beat a dead horse. Or to eat one." He gave a cheeky, knowing smile, and for some reason, this acknowledgment of past traumas set to further calm everyone at the table. I took a sip of my wine. Castillo chuckled, and Dorantes reclined a bit more. Cortés continued. "But in all seriousness, I've met many men who had to learn this lesson the hard way. They show dominance over the masses without any strategic purpose, expecting to be seen as powerful. When the events come to light, and they're reprimanded by those in actual power, they have no idea why. They think their show of force is enough to justify the fallout." Cortés leaned forward, resting his elbow against the table. He looked to each of us now as he spoke. "Your Captain Alcaraz is one of those men. I heard what he did; there was no good reason for it. Now, our host Díaz is a good man; but if your tribe had been a legitimate threat, I doubt he would have reprimanded the captain so harshly. Alcaraz is a fool. He didn't know the lay of the land before he struck."

We sat silently for a moment. Cortés shook his head, still dwelling on the captain's foolishness. I hadn't heard the recent massacre spoken of so casually before. I did not like it.

"You're certainly right, Hernando, in that the tribe posed no threat," I said, poised. "They never took violence against a Spaniard, and they were cooperative; in fact, they led us back here and were caring hosts the entire way."

"Hmm, yes, of course," Cortés said. "They were not a threat in terms of violence, or land or resources... or even the general mood of the indís. Those are the things you have to consider."

I wanted to respond, but I could think of nothing. These were not considerations I knew Cortés had applied to his conquest of Nueva España; my initial role model was changing before my eyes. His ambitions sounded less like an adventure and more like a game of chess. Instead of the lures which drove me to La Florida, I was reminded of the same social ladders I had dreaded to climb in the offices of Sevilla. Where was the man I longed to become? The realization dawned: my ambitions had been drawn up in a fashion that never truly existed. Had I thrown away my true accomplishments in the wilderness?

My stomach suddenly hurt. Perhaps I drank too much wine, but perhaps my thoughts had caused it. I chose to believe my pain was from both the wine *and* the disillusion. Whatever it was, I needed to retreat.

"I've grown quite tired tonight," I said, looking at my companions. "If you'll excuse me... it's been lovely to finally meet you, Hernando."

"Likewise," Cortés said. "It's a good sign, your tiredness. It means that an adventure has been fulfilled." He widened a thin-lipped smile.

I rose to retreat. Hernando Cortés had deemed my time under his sun to end.

CHAPTER 30

Last Conversation
of the Frontier

—

ANDRÉS DORANTES

San Miguel de Culiacán, May 10ᵗʰ, 1536

Alonso del Castillo went to bed shortly after Núñez did. "I think the wine has gotten to me," he said. "I wonder if Alvar felt the same."

Hernando made a suggestion to me after Castillo left. "You aren't drunk yet, are you?"

"No, not yet," I said.

"Why don't we head to Díaz's cellar and open another bottle or two?" Hernando Cortés gave an expectedly cheeky grin.

"I do like the sound of that," I said. "It's been a while since I've had the opportunity to indulge."

We walked through the open hall, now darkened by night, and down the set of nicely-finished stairs to Melchor Díaz's cellar.

"Let's make sure to leave our host the best of his spoils," Cortés said. "But I do see a 1504 Monastrell that could do the trick." He grabbed it from the rack. "Ah, it's from Valencia! No wonder they gave this drink such a pointless name. Name it one thing and you offend Castilla; name it another and you anger Aragón. I do not envy a Valencian winemaker."

"I've never been," I said, but the passion to his story somehow made me feel included in a secret. I now wanted to see the city of Valencia firsthand.

"Don't bother if you haven't," Cortés said, pouring a glass for both me and himself. "There's nothing in Iberia you can't replicate more desirably here."

"Thank you," I said, grabbing the glass. "Is that so?"

Hernando chuckled. "Yes. You can make your own wine and name it whatever you like. There's no age-old feud to force you into compliance." He led me over to the two chairs in the cellar, placed near the entrance, and we sat to relax. "I tell you, once they ship more jamón Ibérico out here, there will be no reason whatsoever to return to Spain."

I listened silently for a moment, somewhat in disbelief that I was drinking wine with my late brother's hero. Despite his distaste for remaining in Spain, he otherwise did not feel quite like what Diego had idealized. I liked him a whole lot more than I thought I would.

"What I'm worried about, Hernando," I finally said, "is that I don't have the money to pay for a vineyard. I have an interesting story; it might lead to some recognition, yes, but that's about all."

"A good story can be sold, too," he said with certitude. "But if you're already questioning that route, I'd advise against it. Writers waste time trying to explain what they can't control." Cortés took a long sip of the Monastrell and nodded to himself. "It's better to have them write about you anyways. Or better yet, to be such a fact of life that they feel writing about your worth is redundant: it should already be known by everyone. And those times when you need people to remain blissfully ignorant, you can rest easy in the fact that they think they know you. You've built your persona."

I had little clue what exactly Cortés meant, but it nonetheless felt instinctively vital, and I held onto it for later deciphering.

"I might've been well-regarded if my father had left me his land. I would have inherited his connections, too," I said, remorseful. Hernando's face dropped from what looked like mild disappointment. I backtracked. "But it's no use complaining. He left me his slave, after all, who's been very useful. Helped save us a few times, I must admit."

"Ah, so the morisco is yours?" he asked. I had piqued his interest.

"Yes," I said. "He was a good friend to my brother, though I suppose that role has passed."

"Sell him."

"What?" I asked, letting my glass slip further toward the ground.

"You should sell him," Hernando repeated, "and use the money to buy a vineyard. Or rather, to buy gifts for a young widow who already owns one. Dress nicely; get her to marry you. There are so many left over from the early days, and they're still young enough to bring you some children."

I struggled to think of a response. "I see… I never realized that."

"Of course not," Cortés said. "Nobody ever thinks about this place like they would the old world. They assume everything is 'new,' and that they won't get the same advantage by taking the same steps they would have at home." Cortés finished the last drink of wine in his glass. He sighed, satisfied. "None of this is new. It's just at the beginning stages, is all. If you're longing for a vineyard, then here it is; but you better get it fast. Take my advice: build yourself well into this society, and trust that it is no different than home. Pretty soon you'll be so entrenched that they don't even know you're here."

Cortés had struck a nerve. I finally understood what he was saying. I took a long last drink of my wine, thinking to myself how this could be one glass of many.

I hesitated, but I knew what was required to buy the life I always wanted. "Where do I sell him?" I asked.

"I have a friend named Coronado," he said. "He might want your Moor for an expedition he's running up north."

With that we grabbed more wine.

CHAPTER 31

A Night in the Town

———

ALONSO DEL CASTILLO

San Miguel de Culiacán, May 10th, 1536

I could think of nothing but rest. A room had been set aside for me to share with Núñez, across from where Dorantes and Estevanico were staying. With slow feet, I walked through the door and over the wood flooring toward my bedside.

Núñez was lying on his bed, across from mine, staring at the ceiling.

"Had enough conversation?" he asked.

I shrugged. "Yeah, it set me a little on edge." I stopped at the foot of my bed for a moment. "I don't know about you, Alvar, but I'm starting to feel like our work here might not amount to much."

"Me too," Alvar Núñez said, his eyes still fixed upward.

"Cortés had me worried," I said. "If he's right about Díaz, in that he isn't as philanthropic as he makes himself out, then I doubt there's anyone else here who'll help us do some good."

Núñez nodded solemnly. "Even still, I'm not positive we're going about this the right way. I mean, we've experienced a lot, but maybe not enough to really 'do some good.' There's too much I don't like about this place. It seems transplanted."

"Interesting," I said, observing his thoughts at work. "I don't feel quite as strongly. But I do understand you perfectly."

There was a pregnant pause in the room. I studied the tiled wall pattern and wondered how much of the material had been shipped from other colonies. Probably the majority, I assumed.

"It's not comfortable," Núñez finally said.

I turned to him. "What isn't?"

He dragged himself upright, scratching the back of his mutilated head. "The bed's not comfortable. I'm drowning in the mattress."

Somewhat confused, I pulled my sheets back and crawled into bed. I laid back, trying to rest and shut my eyes... The bed was certainly comfortable. "I don't know what you mean," I told him.

Soon my head started to fall into the plush of the pillow, and as I drifted, I could not help but notice the soft bag of feathers swallowing me whole; after a minute, my head began to throb.

"Wait, you're right. I can't fall asleep like this."

Núñez mumbled. "I told you. There's no way."

Not long passed until I was standing again, facing the wall. Neither of us were used to the home, or the housemaid, or the new clothing; something about the touch of cotton and silk against my skin was like leather to the tongue, impossible to stomach. And being there, in a place I had dreamed of reaching for so long, I doubted I could ever stomach it. I felt stripped of the solace I had found in God's free earth.

So despite the beds, we slept on the floorboards, and it was the best sleep I'd had in years.

CHAPTER 32

At the End of Life

ALVAR NÚÑEZ
Spain, 1558

I put down the pen and set aside the paper. I have served my time.

The incredible quality of my story gained me a governorship of my own. I was Governor Alvar Núñez of La Plata, southeast of the Incas. With newfound passion, I hoped to scrape together some livable version of a New World. Maybe what I had discovered over years could be put to use if I placed myself at the colonial forefront. But soon, society built around me and—like a rot—it enveloped what I wished to do for the last frontier. The same mistakes became the same standards, and the direction of life I missed was lost once more. Worse still, they could see it in my eyes; the Spaniards knew how I conferred with the indígenas, how I considered their insights valuable. The Spaniards cruelly disconnected me from my source of fulfillment, resigning me to several years in an Andalucían prison. I was back home, but my heart was forever dead. There was no more for me to learn and no more for me to accomplish; with the time I did have, I was not positive I had done right.

But now, I am released. How will I spend my years, and what will my story gain me? My account is not enough to warrant fame, or respect, or the chance to undo the wrongs done against me. The story only curries me enough favor to receive an administrative job for a Duke on the Iberian Peninsula's southern edge. I stack papers at a similar desk to the one I fled thirty years ago. I feel the same nagging pain of what could be.

I check the obituaries one day. My wife's name is María Marmolejo de Velázquez. She has stolen from her neighbor the love of a horseman; as a false widow, she has married a man I mistook to have journeyed with me. She has given life to three children. She lies dead in the unmarked field of a house that is not my own.

I wonder how to leave this world fondly. It seems impossible; I doubt if similar men can later face a different result. Will there ever be another chance to set a new world's course from the beginning?

My hopes for the frontier would undoubtedly require the same complete destruction today's men enacted. So instead, I question whether my life can be seen as the brief, profound meeting that it was. There was an unrepeatable exchange of existences in my short years. I do not want it to be lost.

Regardless, I am unable to pass on my insights. No one I know has come close to understanding what exactly lies across the ocean. Herds of people hear the same calls that beckoned me, though not the sobered voice which returned from the brink. My words come out distorted. I lie awake trying to reconcile what has happened to me and to the many faces I once saw. I want to root out the restlessness that often causes me to stray; still it remains. Selfish ambitions still prevail.

There is a beauty to what I witnessed. I have hidden it beneath doubt and sorrow, and yet it often returns to greet me. My legacy, my hopes, and my worries have all faded, but I remember what is truly good. I must retain it for when the world forgets to.

Acknowledgments

There were many people who made this book a possibility, whether through direct or indirect support. I want to take a moment to mention them all.

To Dad, Mom, Mia, and Colin, you are the best family I could ask for. This process has taken many years, but you encouraged and guided me through all of it. *Iberian Claim* certainly grew up under your loving care. To Chiara, your help was fundamental in making this book what it is. I am in many ways indebted to your thoughtful advice, your patient support, and your words of kindness. Thank you endlessly.

I especially want to thank Gramma, the Crowleys, the Cockrofts, Grant & Lydia, Mary Godmother, the Cascianis, the Barrys, and the Fields. I am so blessed to have you as family. Conor, thanks for spurring my creativity and being my brother.

Thanks to Mazen, Luca, Jason, Shad, Trevor, Bryan, Caden, Lennox, Waylon, Jackson, David, Brett, Dane, Andy, Ian, Owen, Kade, Daniel, Evan, and all my other

Long Beach friends and teammates. To Gabe, Tariq, and Francesco Marron, I had to put this in here.

Thanks also to Jake, Nick, Orion, Anand, Carter, Yusuf, Vamsi, Tanner, Abhir, Ian, Foster, the Cunninghams, the Vances, Bayside Water Polo, Bus 7/581, and my other Virginia Beach friends.

To Eric, Ben, Michael, Deisy, and Will, thanks for being great roommates. I'm also grateful for my UC San Diego, TTV, Zero Gravity Management, and ULC friends and colleagues.

To my teachers and coaches, you've inspired me profoundly. A special thanks to Kenneth Poe.

Aleph Tav.

Without New Degree Press, *Iberian Claim* would not have been possible. I'm grateful to Donovan for introducing me, and to Eric for welcoming me at such a late stage. Brian, the publishing community you have built at NDP is astounding. Colin, you have been the best guide through this entire process; your feedback, wisdom, and positive reinforcement have been invaluable. Mohan, your developmental feedback was likewise imperative. Christy, Venus, and Jamie, I am very appreciative for all your help at many points over these past several months. I am impressed and grateful for the hard work of both Erica's video editing team and Gjorji's cover design team. Thank you also to the layout team, copy-editing team, and everyone else at NDP involved in making *Iberian Claim* the best it could be.

My acknowledgments would be incomplete without appreciation for the beta readers who provided their time and effort. Megan, I am honored by the amount of care you put into such careful feedback; your thoroughness improved my edits tremendously. Aunt Karen, Gramma, Mom, and Dad, I am equally thankful for your honest and informative suggestions. Though the scheduling did not align, I'm also grateful to Courtney, Lisa & Abby, Mrs. Carbonara, Mrs. Satariano, Mr. Campatelli, and Mr. Arzate for their willingness to help.

To everyone who pre-ordered, you made this book a reality. You are an amazing community of people, and I am floored to have received your support:

Mazen Abouelela

Bryan Aguirre

Veronica Almodovar

Megan & Dave Barry

Mia & Colin Barry

Eric Boone

Dorothy & John Calley

Matthew & Kristin Casciani

Roger & Edith Casciani

Thomas & Catherine Casciani

Lindy, April, Lucas, Travis & Janet Cockroft

Karen & Tim Crowley

Tom & MJ Daues

Jill & Phil Dietz

Sue Harrison

Caden Elsesser

Luca Emerson

Erin Fekjar

Kelly Ferguson

Jeremiah Fernandez

Carrie & George Fields

Ariel Fields

Chiara Fields

Gabriel Fields

Benjamin Garfinkel

Hank Gentile

Paul Gentile

Cranston Gittens

The Gurich Family

Luca Pfeiffer

Andrew Hendricks

Andy Hernandez

Ellen & Eugene Ichinose

Laura Kielbowicz

Eric Koester

Marie Kolpak

Carson Krueger

Prisha Kukkal

Emily Ladewig

Nosa Lawani

Ryan Leroux

Jake Levine

Emily T. Long

Mark Lucas

Kelly Ma

Suzan Mahdai

Ariella & Mariana Markouizos

Lisa Martin

Deisy Martinez

Todd Masot

Ann Matika

Ian McGary

Ryan Nakano

Shane Nantais

Marcia Nye

Caroline Parrinello

Kara Pedersen

Fr. Scott & Dawn Pederson

Ken & Midge Pellegrino

Lynda Peoples

Maggie Polite

Sam Polite

Jackson Prosser

Hannah Rigazzi

Liberty Romanik

Natasha Spangrud

Quiana Stodder

Jeanette & Ned Turner

J. Benjamin Unkle, Jr.

Joseph Uribe

David Vandevert

Dane Vangilder

Angelina Verdugo

Jean Mackay Vinson

Alan Wachob

Farsamin Warisha

Kade Margain

Eve Wittenmyer

Daryl Woodard

Patty Williams

Ava Zell

This book is also dedicated to the loving memories of Uncle Ben Cockroft, Latham Bell, Mrs. Chang, Aunt Kami, and Nana.

Research and Sources

———

Iberian Claim is certainly not a direct adaptation of Álvar Núñez Cabeza de Vaca's account. However, Núñez provided much of the historical background necessary for developing the characters, events, and atmosphere of the book. As a result, *Iberian Claim* is less historical fiction and more of a fiction based on and in critique of a primary source. Though the biases and opportunities for falsehood are increased when relying heavily on a primary source, Núñez wrote the sole surviving chronicle of the expedition and gave an insightful look into the period as a whole (as far as colonialism is concerned). However, this does not mean that other sources were not employed, and many are named here. First, though, is the citation for Núñez's account:

Cabeza De Vaca, Alvar Núñez. *Chronicle of the Narváez Expedition*. Edited by Harold Augenbraum. Translated by Fanny Bandelier. New York: Penguin, 2002.

The other preparatory research was done only so that the book would feel more authentic, and so that readers in turn could better picture the various stakes involved with colonization. This list is not comprehensive, but does show a range for the supplementary sources used:

"16th C Spain. Overview: Politics." *Spain Then and Now,* 2009. https://www.spainthenandnow.com/spanish-history/16th-c-spain-overview-politics.

Chipman, Donald E. "CABEZA DE VACA, ALVAR NUNEZ." *Handbook of Texas Online,* Texas State Historical Association, June 12, 2010. Modified March 9, 2012. http://www.tshaonline.org/handbook/online/articles/fca06.

Chipman, Donald E. "CASTILLO MALDONADO, ALONSO." *Handbook of Texas Online,* Texas State Historical Association, June 12, 2010. http://www.tshaonline.org/handbook/online/articles/fcaaz.

Chipman, Donald E. "DORANTES DE CARRANZA, ANDRES." *Handbook of Texas Online,* Texas State Historical Association, June 12, 2010. http://www.tshaonline.org/handbook/online/articles/fdo20.

Chipman, Donald E. "ESTEVANICO." *Handbook of Texas Online,* Texas State Historical Association, June 12, 2010. Modified November 5, 2013. http://www.tshaonline.org/handbook/online/articles/fes08.

"Galveston, Texas Museums." *Texas Tourism & Marketing,* Galveston.com & Company, 2015.

Grant, Richard. "Cabeza De Vaca - Cowboys and Indians Magazine." *Cowboys and Indians Magazine,* August 18, 2015. https://www.cowboysindians.com/2015/08/cabeza-de-vaca/.

"Hernando Cortés." *BBC News,* 2014. http://www.bbc.co.uk/history/historic_figures/cortes_hernan.shtml.

Hickman, Kennedy. "War of the League of Cambrai: Battle of Ravenna." *About.com Military History,* 2014.

Johnson, John G. "NARVAEZ, PANFILO DE." *Handbook of Texas Online,* Texas State Historical Association, June 15, 2010. http://www.tshaonline.org/handbook/online/articles/fna22.

Machiavelli, Niccolò. *The Prince.* Translated by Tim Parks. New York: Penguin, 2009.

"Native American Tribes of Florida." *Florida Indian Tribes and Languages,* Native Languages of the Americas, n.d. Accessed December 28, 2016. http://www.native-languages.org/florida.htm.

"Sonora." *History.com,* A&E Television Networks, December 7, 2009. www.history.com/topics/mexico/sonora.

Walbert, David. "Spain and America: From Reconquest to Conquest." Learn NC, 2007. http://www.davidwalbert.com/pdf/learnnc/spain-and-america-from-reconquest-p1677.pdf.

Below, I am leaving a few works for **suggested reading**. The first book mentioned is one I have yet to read, due to a belief that it would sap my creativity and present a possibility for unintentional plagiarism. Nevertheless, this novel has sold well and is very highly regarded. Here's a dramatized account focusing specifically on Estevanico and a Moroccan perspective:

The Moor's Account by Laila Lalami

A couple other books which guided my thinking:

Atlas of Indian Nations by Anton Truer

The Prince by Niccolò Machiavelli

Leonardo da Vinci by Walter Isaacson

Lastly, I must recommend the show *Survivor* for those who love social dynamics in survival-like settings.